Northwest TREASURE

PRESENTED TO:

Northwest TREASURE

A PHOTOGRAPHIC PORTRAIT OF
TACOMA–PIERCE COUNTY

Northwest TREASURE

Editor in Chief	Rob Levin
Publisher	Barry Levin
Associate Publishers	Bob Sadoski, John Lorenzo
Chamber of Commerce Liaison	Sonja Hall
Senior Editor	Renée Peyton
Project Director	Cheryl Sadler
Photo Editor	Jill Dible
Project Coordinator	Muriel Diguette
Writers	Kimberly DeMeza, Rena Distasio, Grace Hawthorne, Regina Roths
Copy Editor	Bob Land
Book Design	Compōz Design, LLC
Jacket Design	Kevin Smith
Prepress	Vickie Berdanis
Photographers	Jim Bryant, Eric Francis, David Gibb, Jackson Hill, Alan Weiner

RIVERBEND BOOKS
A division of BOOKHOUSE GROUP, INC.

Published by Riverbend Books
an Imprint of Bookhouse Group, Inc.
818 Marietta Street, NW
Atlanta, Georgia 30318
www.riverbendbooks.net
404.885.9515

Library of Congress Cataloging-in-Publication Data

Northwest treasure : a photographic portrait of Tacoma–Pierce County / editor, Rob Levin. — 1st ed.
p. cm.
ISBN 1-883987-27-X (alk. paper)
1. Tacoma (Wash.)—Pictorial works. 2. Pierce County (Wash.)—Pictorial works. 3. Tacoma (Wash.)—Description and travel. 4. Pierce County (Wash.)—Description and travel. 5. Tacoma (Wash.)—Economic conditions. 6. Pierce County (Wash.)—Economic conditions. 7. Business enterprises—Washington (State)—Tacoma. 8. Business enterprises—Washington (State)—Pierce County. I. Levin, Rob, 1955-
F899.T2N67 2006
979.7'788—dc22
2006020574

According to a survey conducted by the Point Defiance Park Revitalization Plan, 80 percent of those responding rated Five Mile Drive as the most popular draw of the park. The route winds through the Point's old-growth forest and offers spectacular views of Puget Sound, the Cascade and Olympic mountain ranges, Tacoma Narrows and Narrows Bridge, Vashon Island, and Gig Harbor. On Saturday mornings the park is closed to vehicles so visitors can run, walk, or bicycle along the drive undisturbed. As landscape architect Sydney Hare, who created the park's initial master plan, said, "Probably no other city in this country has such a beautiful natural park. Its setting and relation to the city are unique and ideal." ∎

It is only natural that the Jack Hyde Park located on the water's edge in the Old Town area is named in memory of Jack Hyde, former Tacoma mayor and a leader in the development of the park and the Ruston Way waterfront. The plaza below the grassy area in the park is a great place to enjoy the view. If you decide to take a walk along Ruston Way and are coming by boat, you can tie up at the Old Town Dock and take advantage of the picnic tables, covered shelters, beaches, and restrooms in nearby Dickman Mill Park, which was the site of the old Dickman Lumber Mill, acquired by Metro Parks in the early 1990s. About the time you've walked enough to need a drink of water, you'll find one at Hamilton Park. Then it's on to Les Davis Pier, which offers fishing and easy access to concessions and a skate rental shop, which is open in the summer. It is also the starting point for many divers because it is the site of an artificial reef. And what waterfront trail would be complete without a beach, which you will find at Marine Park on the south end of Ruston Way. ■

Table of Contents

The unique cable-stay-designed State Route 509 Bridge is a vital component of the Tacoma Renaissance, carrying thousands of people a day over the Thea Foss Waterway between Interstate 5 and downtown Tacoma. At one end of the Foss lies Ruston Way, a series of narrow shoreline parks that provide numerous recreational opportunities along Commencement Bay. At the other end are the newly redeveloped areas of downtown that include such landmarks as the Union Station federal courthouse and the Museum of Glass, International Center for Contemporary Art, whose unique stainless-steel hot-shop cone can be seen here to the left in the foreground. ■

Foreword

A wonderful experience awaits you as you journey through this book, which showcases some of the fascinating people, places, and happenings that make Tacoma–Pierce County one of the Pacific Northwest's most sought-after destinations.

More than 755,000 diverse residents have fallen in love with Pierce County, and make its cities and towns their homes. From historic Tacoma to industrial Frederickson, tech-savvy Dupont to the bedroom community of University Place, residents enjoy a quality of life many agree is unmatched. An overriding sense of welcome for businesses, individuals, and families offers newcomers metro- and cosmopolitan amenities while providing warm hometown charm.

We are a rapidly emerging region celebrated for setting benchmarks among mid-sized cities for revitalization and creative economic growth strategies. Our thriving economy remains stable through national economic cycles, due in large part to the presence of two of our nation's most important military installations, McChord Air Force Base and award-winning Fort Lewis. Tacoma–Pierce County is also home to unique infrastructure and intermodal transportation efficiency through the Port of Tacoma, a major gateway for trade to Asia and Alaska. Our prosperity is also attributed to quality education opportunities, top-ranking health-care facilities, and an abundance of natural resources.

Tacoma–Pierce County is one of the Northwest's prime travel destinations. We are home to a vibrant arts community, large-scale events, acclaimed museums, a large zoo and aquarium, new and refurbished event venues, world-class spas, new hotels, fine dining, hip night life, lively entertainment, and attractive retail centers. All offer something valuable to see and do around every corner.

Perhaps one of Tacoma–Pierce County's best-kept secrets is its unique central proximity to a wide variety of outdoor recreational opportunities and easy access to neighboring communities. Within about thirty minutes in any direction are activities offered on Puget Sound, to the east at Mount Rainier and the Cascade Mountain range, to the west at the Olympic Mountains, in the northern city of Seattle, and Washington State's capital of Olympia just south of Pierce County. Thanks to our moderate climate, most activities and attractions can be enjoyed year-round.

It is my hope that you will take a few moments to sit down, relax, and enjoy a peek into our lives, and at some of the many interesting places that make our community a vibrant place to live, work, play, and do business. On behalf of its residents, I welcome you to Tacoma–Pierce County, notably "one of America's most livable" and treasured communities.

David W. Graybill, CCE, CEcD
President & CEO, Tacoma–Pierce County Chamber

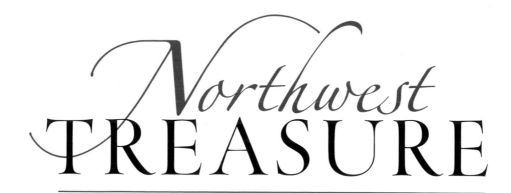

Northwest TREASURE

**would not have been possible without
the support of the following sponsors:**

Columbia Bank ■ Comfor Products Incorporated ■ Courtyard by Marriott Downtown Tacoma
■ Key Bank ■ King Oscar/Tacoma Inn, Motels & Convention Centers ■ LeMay Enterprises, Inc.
■ Pierce County Public Works & Utilities ■ Tacoma-Pierce County Chamber ■ Tacoma Public Utilities

SUBWAY

HARMON BREWERY

SUNDAY
ALL YOU CAN EAT
FISH & CHIPS
$9.95

HARMON LOFTS

NOW
OPEN
INDOCHINE

Tacoma is teeming with things to do, places to go, and people to meet. Pedestrian-friendly, the city offers a number of museums, galleries, retail shops, and restaurants all within walking distance from one another. The Washington State History Museum on downtown's bustling Pacific Street is just waiting to be explored, as are the Museum of Glass, International Center for Contemporary Art, and the Tacoma Art Museum just around the corner. Tacoma's waterfront on Commencement Bay of Puget Sound is also a great place for wandering around by foot or by rollerblade. ∎

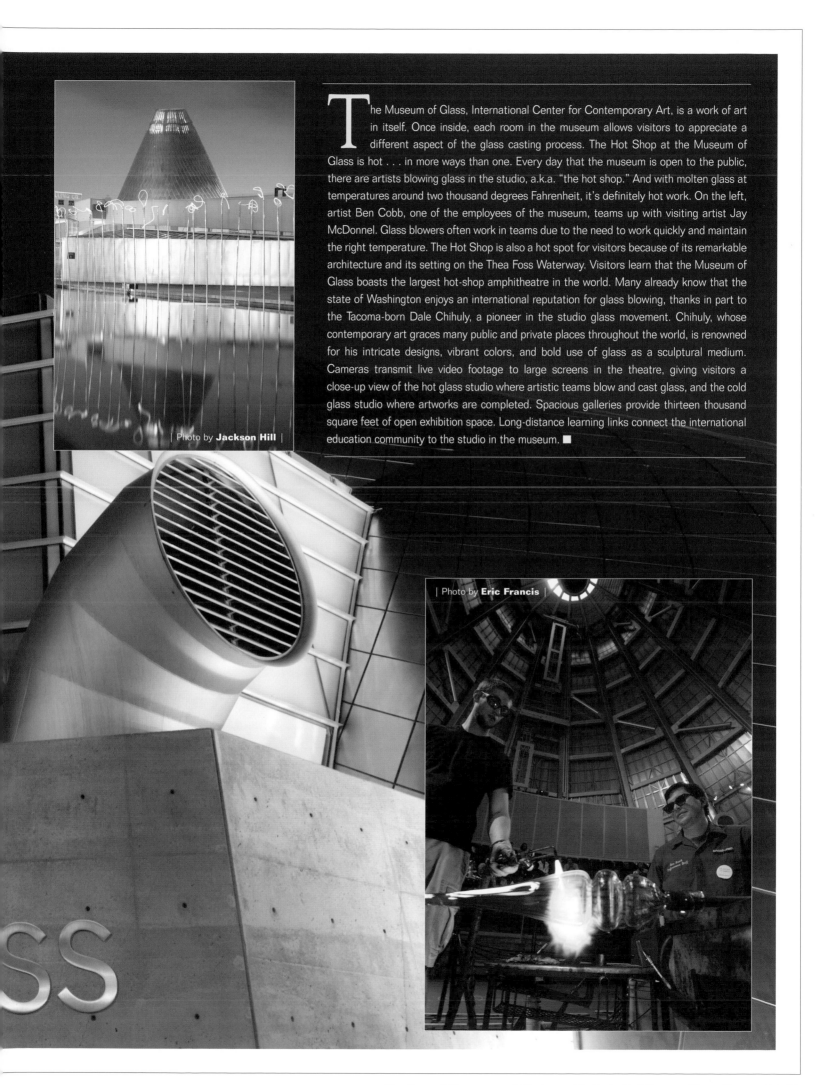

Tthe Museum of Glass, International Center for Contemporary Art, is a work of art in itself. Once inside, each room in the museum allows visitors to appreciate a different aspect of the glass casting process. The Hot Shop at the Museum of Glass is hot . . . in more ways than one. Every day that the museum is open to the public, there are artists blowing glass in the studio, a.k.a. "the hot shop." And with molten glass at temperatures around two thousand degrees Fahrenheit, it's definitely hot work. On the left, artist Ben Cobb, one of the employees of the museum, teams up with visiting artist Jay McDonnel. Glass blowers often work in teams due to the need to work quickly and maintain the right temperature. The Hot Shop is also a hot spot for visitors because of its remarkable architecture and its setting on the Thea Foss Waterway. Visitors learn that the Museum of Glass boasts the largest hot-shop amphitheatre in the world. Many already know that the state of Washington enjoys an international reputation for glass blowing, thanks in part to the Tacoma-born Dale Chihuly, a pioneer in the studio glass movement. Chihuly, whose contemporary art graces many public and private places throughout the world, is renowned for his intricate designs, vibrant colors, and bold use of glass as a sculptural medium. Cameras transmit live video footage to large screens in the theatre, giving visitors a close-up view of the hot glass studio where artistic teams blow and cast glass, and the cold glass studio where artworks are completed. Spacious galleries provide thirteen thousand square feet of open exhibition space. Long-distance learning links connect the international education community to the studio in the museum. ■

| Photo by **Jackson Hill** |

| Photo by **Eric Francis** |

| Photo by **Eric Francis** |

Cannon Construction: Leader in Telecommunications Solutions

P owered by a single backhoe and an entrepreneurial spirit, Mike Cannon dug the foundation for a successful niche contracting business in 1985. Today Cannon Construction, Inc. is a diversified telecommunications contractor, providing copper, data, and fiber cabling systems for corporations and government agencies around the world.

"By focusing on turnkey telecommunication solutions we've been able to provide our customers with the cutting-edge service they need to remain competitive well into the twenty-first century," says Cannon, president and CEO.

While much of the work completed by Cannon Construction is less than obvious to the eye, all of the work is integral to the efficient operations of businesses, city governments, and military bases. For example, in a recent telecommunications upgrade, one area military installation's training center needed to interface its 844 computers in various buildings. Cannon Construction executed the project, which included more than fifty-two miles of computer cable. The company's core services include Inside Plant (ISP) and Outside Plant (OSP). ISP services include

> *"The quality of our people, and the quality of the work we perform—that's what keeps our business going strong."*

information management systems; premise wiring; specialized voice, video, and high-speed data cabling; LAN/WAN systems; and fiber and copper cable splicing. OSP services include telecommunications infrastructure upgrades, site surveys and design, trenching, duct banks, manholes, rock sawing, directional drilling, cable blowing and pulling, splicing, testing, terminating, and real-time Kinematic GPS surveying. In addition to nationwide telecommunications services, Cannon Construction is a preferred contractor for a number of public and private corporations, utility co-ops, commercial developers, and municipalities in the Pacific Northwest. This division specializes in site work, demolition, utilities, water distribution systems, and sub-metering.

Above all, the application of telecommunications infrastructure and utility solutions demands a quality foundation. The same can be said for Cannon Construction. "The quality of our people, and the quality of the work we perform—that's what keeps our business going strong," explains Cannon. In addition to quality, the company is also known for its exemplary safety record, its precision teamwork, and its integrity. These principles have not only guided the company to the successful industry leadership position it holds today, they have been instrumental in forming a company that is an attractive place to work. Among forty public and private companies, ranging from small to large, Cannon Construction ranked second in South Puget Sound's Top Places to Work awards program. "As this recognition is based on the qualities of solidarity, equity, integrity, appreciation, and gratification as viewed by the employees, it is extremely meaningful to us," says Cannon. "It means we walk our talk, and we work not only as a team, but as a family." From one man with one backhoe and a big dream, to a diverse company of more than 150 employees managing multimillion-dollar projects, Cannon Construction exemplifies the relationship between solid foundation and success. ■

Cannon Construction is proud to be a preferred contractor providing best-value solutions to various Department of Defense agencies around the globe.

| Photo by **Eric Francis** |

| Photo by **Eric Francis** |

Thanks to Eulalie Wagner, wife of George Corydon Wagner and distinguished member of the Board of Directors of the Garden Club of America in the mid-1960s, everyone in Tacoma has a country retreat to visit to get a reprieve from the hustle and bustle of city living. In 1987, this renowned landscape garden enthusiast donated her entire ten-acre estate, Lakewold, complete with a Georgian revival–style manor and its breathtaking gardens, to the nonprofit Friends of Lakewold. Her aim was to preserve the beautiful environment found at the estate, which has become a bona fide crown jewel of the Lakes District. The estate, built in the early 1900s and now known as Lakewold Gardens, features a plethora of picturesque gardens, from the Rose Garden, Fern Garden, and Woodland Garden to the Rhododendron Collection, Boxwood Parterres, and Screes. Located along the west shore of Gravelly Lake, Lakewold Gardens is a haven nestled in woods with an outstanding view of Mount Rainier and garden design by celebrated landscape architect Thomas Church. The list of owners of the estate, dating back to 1908, reads like a who's who of Tacoma society, and today's visitors are able to enjoy a glimpse of the lifestyle savored by some of the area's most esteemed residents. Open year-round and offering self-guided walking tours, Lakewold Gardens is the perfect destination for everyone who wants to spend some time with Mother Nature. ■

Lakewood Clinic physician
Dr. Jennifer Edgoose is dedicated to infant care. As family-practice specialists Community Health provides a wide range of medical services covering every stage of life, from newborns to seniors. Even teenagers have their own clinic, located at Eastside in Tacoma.

| Photo by **Eric Francis** |

Community Health Care Provides Compassionate Care to All

One of the most pressing issues facing health-care workers in the modern age is how best to provide quality care for society's underserved populations. Recognizing the inadequacy of resources for low-income patients in their own area, in 1969 a group of concerned Pierce County community leaders and physicians met to create a solution.

A year later, Community Health Care opened its doors, with two volunteer clinics and a mission to provide quality, compassionate care accessible to all. Today, that mission is still going strong, as Community Health Care provides over thirty-five thousand patients annually with high-quality, family-practice-style care.

"Our goal is to provide care for the long term, on a preventative, not just emergency, basis," says president and CEO David Flentge. "We want to be our patients' medical and dental home." Medical Care is currently provided at eight full-service clinics—three in Tacoma, two in Lakewood, and one each in Parkland, Sumner, and Spanaway. Dental services are provided at three clinics in Lakewood and Tacoma, one of which is specifically geared toward children. Additional clinics specialize in internal medicine (Lakewood) and a Health Care for the Homeless Clinic in downtown Tacoma.

> *"Our goal is to provide care for the long term, on a preventative, not just emergency, basis."*

Also part of Community Health Care's services are three full pharmacies, three satellite pharmacies with automated dispensing machines, a maternity support program, a senior foot care clinic, and mental health services in conjunction with Greater Lakes Mental Healthcare.

In addition to twenty-eight medical and fourteen dental providers, Community Health Care employs outreach workers to provide support services including specialist referrals and assistance with public or subsidized medical insurance program applications. Outreach workers also link to a variety of community social service partners—food and clothing banks, low-cost housing providers, and so on—that fulfill another vital component of total patient care.

Services are provided to the uninsured on a sliding-fee scale, as well as to those on Medicaid and Medicare. And, because Community Health Care aims to be the provider of choice for all patients seeking high-quality, compassionate care, it also accepts private insurers as well.

A nonprofit organization, Community Health Care is governed by a twenty-one-member board of directors, 51 percent of whom are required to be patients in the organization's clinics. This mix ensures a very active board, which, says Flentge, "not only sees as their vision to provide care for patients, but also to develop community support and collaborative relationships for our long-term success."

Over the years, Community Health Care has developed strong partnerships with the Pierce County Medical Society, the Pierce County Dental Society, and the Community Health Plan of Washington, a statewide insurance plan that contracts with Community Health Care to ensure services to Medicaid and Basic Health Plan patients. The United Way, the county health department, and the cooperation of what Flentge calls "an exceptional hospital system" all contribute vital monetary support and/or partnerships.

"Basically, this is about many good people working together with a shared vision," says Flentge. "Board and staff are concerned first and foremost not about with what's good for the organization, but with what's good for our patients and their families." ■

Each year Community Health provides high-quality dental services to tens of thousands of noninsured patients. Dentists like Wilfredo Garay, DDS, of the Lakewood Dental Clinic focus on preventative and restorative services for patients of all ages and on early screening and sealants for children.

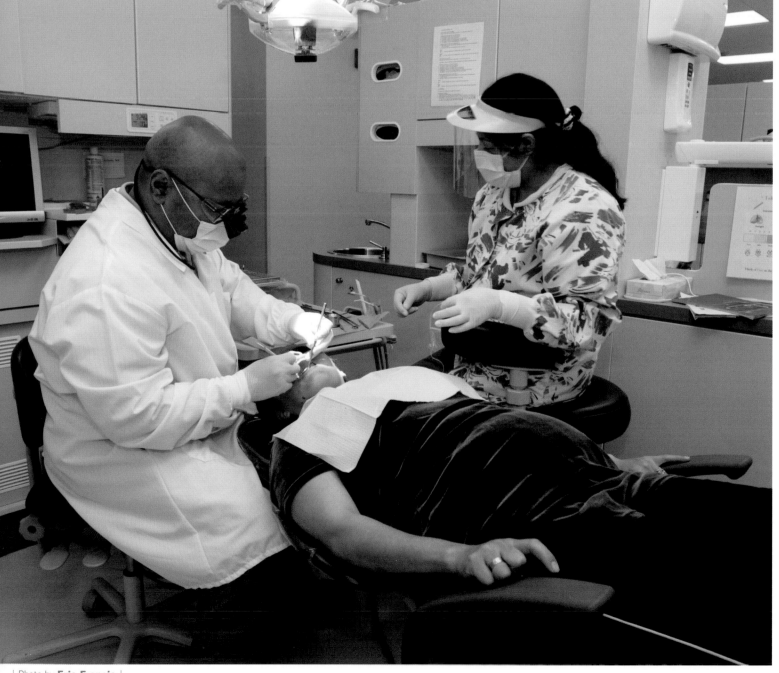

| Photo by **Eric Francis** |

"Homecoming at George R. Curtis Senior High School is probably our largest community event," said Terry Jenks, athletic director and activities coordinator. "Homecoming Assembly, which is held in the gym, has been going on since 1978, and we regularly have twelve hundred parents and alumni who support us." The evening features student games, skits, songs, competitions, and awards. The class with the most sportsmanship and school spirit is always given recognition. Of course, homecoming wouldn't be homecoming without the Vikings football team and a smiling queen, like senior Jamie Georg, to reign over the festivities. Student leaders and teachers make sure there are activities throughout the week. There is always a day to show off the school colors of blue and white and plenty of other opportunities, like Twin Day and Eighties Day, to wear costumes. Curtis High School is located in University Place, a small community west of Tacoma, with a population of 30,500. The area is within an easy commute of ocean beaches and the Cascade Mountains. ∎

Homecoming football!

Rushing up the field toward the red zone with ball securely in hand, this Mount Tahoma High School Thunderbird breaks a tackle as things heat up during the team's homecoming game against the Capital High School Cougars from nearby Olympia. This highly anticipated match-up between these top Narrows League varsity squads always promises to be one of the highlights of the fall football schedule, especially when they meet at Mount Tahoma Stadium. Under the blazing Friday night lights, the players from each team put on quite a show, rousing spectators on both sides of the field with outstanding athleticism and heart-pounding action between the goalposts. And for the Thunderbirds, home-field advantage doesn't mean the team takes anything for granted, as these dedicated athletes play with the same passion whether they're at home or away. For them, what really matters is that when 7:00 p.m. rolls around each week between early September and late October, they're ready to play sixty minutes of outstanding and electrifying football. ■

| Photo by **Eric Francis** |

From asthma and cardiac services to oncology and orthopedics, the newly expanded Mary Bridge Children's Health Center is the region's most complete source of pediatric outpatient care. It is also designed to provide a healing environment for the kids, with plenty of natural light, warm spaces, children-sized furnishings, and playful décor.

MultiCare Health System Dedicated to Family-Focused Care

Because effective patient care is never about just one person or one treatment, the physicians and nurses at MultiCare Health System excel at combining their expertise to bring together the very best in care.

It's an approach that contributes to the well-being of thousands of patients each year—like one older gentleman who was worried his knee replacement surgery would prevent him from pursuing his favorite hobby, fly-fishing. But thanks to a personalized treatment plan by MultiCare doctors and physical therapists, he is well on his way to fishing his favorite streams again.

A community-based, nonprofit organization, MultiCare has grown into southwest Washington's premier provider of health-care services. Patients throughout Pierce and south King counties receive services at Allenmore Hospital, Tacoma General Hospital, and Mary Bridge Children's Hospital & Health Center, as well as twenty physician clinics, six urgent-care centers, and specialty clinics in the community.

MultiCare's focus on excellence, innovation, and patient care has earned it both national and local recognition.

With patient- and family-focused care as the primary goal, MultiCare is also distinguished by clinical excellence and ongoing innovations in the latest medical technologies and procedures.

The MultiCare Surgical Care Center and MultiCare Regional Heart & Vascular Center at Tacoma General Hospital is the state's most advanced surgical center and encompasses some of the latest surgical techniques available, including robotic surgery. With a history in the area going back to 1882, Tacoma General is also a leading provider of over a dozen additional specialties, including the only Level III Neonatal Intensive Care Unit in the South Sound region.

Along with its strong medical/surgical focus, the 130-bed Allenmore Hospital offers top-quality care in specialty areas including cancer, neurology, and orthopedics. To better serve its patients, the hospital recently added a new six-bed intensive care unit and expanded its emergency department to serve even more patients.

For children, MultiCare offers the special care of Mary Bridge Children's Hospital & Health Center—the region's only dedicated pediatric hospital and the most complete resource for pediatric outpatient specialty care.

MultiCare's focus on excellence, innovation, and patient care has earned it both national and local recognition, including the 2005 NRC award for top doctors and nurses and the 2005 Verispan Top 100 Integrated Health Care Systems designation.

But its most cherished rewards are the ones that come from the organization's close ties to the community. MultiCare takes leadership roles in hosting a variety of community events, participating in health and wellness activities, and collaborating with organizations like the YMCA and the Tacoma–Pierce County Health Department to improve community health. One of the area's top philanthropic events, the Festival of Trees fund-raiser for Mary Bridge Children's Hospital & Health Center, draws support from hundreds of volunteers who donate thousands of hours.

MultiCare works to make every patient's visit more compassionate and more convenient. In short, they put the community's health first. ■

Serving Tacoma General Hospital and Mary Bridge Children's Hospital, the MultiCare Surgical Care Center and MultiCare Regional Heart & Vascular Center provide advanced technology and care for general, pediatric, and cardiovascular patients. The 169,000-square-foot facility includes twelve operating suites, spacious recovery rooms, private surgeon/family consultation rooms, and comfortable waiting areas.

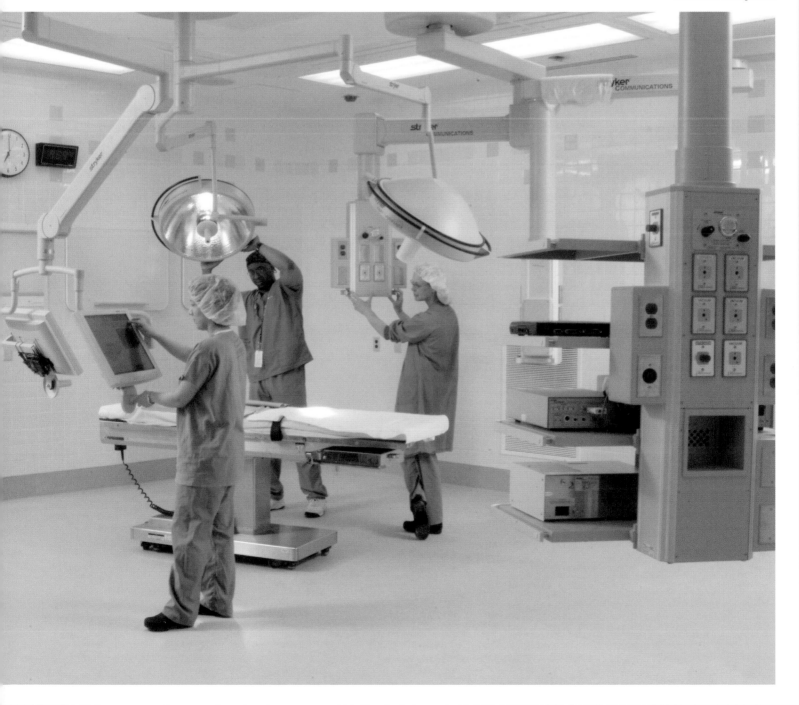

Crystal Mountain Ski Area is aptly named. On a crystal clear day, the view from the summit is an alluring 360-degree panorama of the Cascade Range, including Mount Rainier. In the winter the resort attracts skiers of all abilities with 13 percent beginner, 57 percent intermediate, and 30 percent advanced terrain. But what Crystal Mountain is best known for is its easy-access backcountry terrain for those who prefer the extreme. The entire resort spans twenty-three hundred acres, but nearly half is patrolled, out-of-bounds, ungroomed areas that also offer a quick return to the base area. It's no wonder that Crystal Mountain has continually placed on the top-twenty-five list for ski areas in North America. And when summertime brings warmer temps, the same spectacular views are there for the taking from the summit, as visitors enjoy scenic chair lift rides topped off by a meal at the state's highest restaurant: the Summit House. ∎

Russell Investment Group portfolio managers Derek Leonard, left, and Brian Causey discuss how best to trade stocks on behalf of a large pension fund. Russell provides investment solutions for some two thousand clients in thirty-nine countries.

| Photo by **Eric Francis** |

Russell Investment Group Personally Invested in Success of Clients

What happens when a company spends decades making its associates a top priority? Simple. Everyone—clients, associates, and community alike—wins.

Russell Investment Group, founded as Frank Russell Company in 1936, believes satisfied and empowered associates generate satisfied clients. That corporate culture along with a valuable investment process makes Russell a rapidly growing investment services firm whose purpose is improving financial security for people. As an investment consultant, Russell has $2.3 trillion under advisement. As investment manager, the company manages another $155 billion in assets.

Headquartered in Tacoma, the company has offices in New York, Chicago, San Diego, San Francisco, Milwaukee, Toronto, London, Melbourne, Paris, Singapore, Sydney, Auckland, Tokyo, Johannesburg, Amsterdam, and Geneva. An impressive list . . . as is their client base, which includes AT&T, Compaq, BHP Billiton, General Motors, and JC Penney Co., Inc.

It was George Russell Jr. who took over the company from his grandfather in 1958 and transformed it from a retail brokerage firm to a global provider of research, with a full range of investment services to retirement plans, foundations, endowments, and other financial services and organizations. Russell's comprehensive knowledge of money managers allows it to deliver professional-quality strategies for institutional and individual investors.

> *"Whether associates have been with us two years or twenty years, we hope they feel as if they have a real stake here."*

"George and Jane Russell were the true architects of Russell's culture because he was such a strong innovator and she taught everyone the importance of people within an organization," said Craig Ueland, Russell president and CEO. "Now we have associates all across the company who are building on that legacy of long-term success with an extraordinary value system as its core."

Quality and trust are key ingredients in Russell's overall success. "Whether associates have been with us two years or twenty years, we hope they feel as if they have a real stake here and are personally invested in the success of our clients and each other," says Ueland. "At the same time we want our associates, and therefore our company, to achieve a balance, with a strong place for family and community."

The firm sets aside a growing percentage of its profits for investment in the communities where they do business. They also encourage Russell associates to become involved in the community. "Given that Tacoma is our corporate headquarters," says Fred Kiga, Russell's director of corporate and government relations, "a significant amount of our giving gets invested here."

The primary focus for Russell's corporate giving is helping children and improving financial literacy, but the company supports a wide range of organizations. Recent grants include the Tacoma Art Museum, the Museum of Glass, Pacific Lutheran University, Junior Achievement, and Save the Children. The company is a continuing supporter of the Pierce County Arts Foundation and has recently endowed a chair at the University of Washington, Tacoma.

Financial security, taking care of people and business—it's all in a busy day's work at Russell Investment Group. ∎

Kelly Haughton, strategic director for Russell indexes, advises a student on saving for retirement as part of a Junior Achievement of Washington program on financial decision making for Tacoma eighth-graders. Russell is involved in numerous community-service programs around the world.

| Photo by **Eric Francis** |

As the sun sets behind a fog-shrouded Tacoma Narrows Bridge, all is calm and quiet as cars traverse the fifth-longest suspension bridge in the country. Because of the area's steady growth over the years and the popularity of the bridge, which allows commuters to continue their journey on State Route 16 across the Puget Sound, an initiative to widen the 5,979-foot-long historical structure began in the late 1990s. Construction on a second span of the bridge, sitting parallel to the current bridge, commenced in 2002 under the direction of the Washington State Department of Transportation and Tacoma Narrows Contractors. The $849 million project will be completed in summer 2007, opening up traffic flow over the water by providing much-needed and long-awaited new lanes for eastbound travelers. Once the new span is open to the public, renovations on the current span, which dates back to 1950, will continue, bringing the entire bridge up to the current earthquake code and giving all commuters the comforting knowledge that they will be able to enjoy a safe, comfortable, and convenient ride along the Tacoma Narrows Bridge each and every day. ■

Pacific Lutheran University: Challenge, Support, Success

Pacific Lutheran University (PLU), located in suburban Parkland on a 126-acre woodland campus, offers more than thirty-six hundred students a unique blend of academically rigorous liberal arts and professional programs. At PLU, students develop skills in decision making, analysis, communication, and reasoning that prepare them for a lifetime of success—both in their careers and in service to others.

There are a number of reasons that students choose PLU, including a full range of liberal arts academic programs—such as psychology, history, and the natural sciences—anchored by a college of arts and sciences. The university also provides students the opportunity for professional study in business, education, nursing, social work,

PLU offers a unique blend of academically rigorous liberal arts and professional programs.

and physical education. Each of these programs maintains a strong liberal arts emphasis at its core. Master's degrees are offered in business, education, marriage and family therapy, nursing, and writing. In addition, PLU is committed to developing in all students a global perspective, including an understanding of the intercultural and intellectual richness of the world. More than 40 percent of students spend time studying abroad. Throughout its history PLU has remained closely affiliated with the Lutheran Church.

Given the combination of rigorous academics and a friendly, personalized environment, it's easy to see why PLU is the only university in the Northwest to be listed every year within the top fifteen Western region universities in the Best Colleges survey published annually by *U.S. News & World Report.* ■

Since it first opened in 1913, the Eleventh Street Bridge has had a long and interesting history. The 1,748-foot bridge crosses the Thea Foss Waterway. In 1957, forty-four years after it was constructed, it was rebuilt. Then in 1997 it was renamed as the Murray Morgan Bridge. Morgan was a preeminent historian of the Puget Sound region and wrote much of Skid Road while serving as a bridge tender here. The bridge watched over the passage of vessels during Tacoma's tall ship festival in 2005. However, perhaps its most unusual function was as a nesting place for peregrine falcons. In their natural habitat the falcons nest on cliff faces, but in more recent times they have moved to high bridges and tall buildings in urban areas. A nesting box was added to the bridge to help protect the falcon eggs, and bridge maintenance work scheduled by the Washington State Department of Transportation was halted to wait for two fledglings to take flight. In 2006, the fate of the bridge was uncertain. It was scheduled for demolition, but advocates were working to have it declared a landmark and preserved as a pedestrian and bicycle route. ■

| Photo by **Jim Bryant** |

I t's one of the only social work programs like it in the country, and its therapy isn't about talking; it's about art making. In 1994, glass artist Dale Chihuly helped create Tacoma's Hilltop Artists in Residence glassblowing program at Jason Lee Middle School. The idea was to give disadvantaged youth aged twelve to twenty an alternative to life on the streets and to encourage them to stay in school. Since then the hot shop has served hundreds of youth with its classes, held thirteen hours a day, five days a week. Instead of getting into trouble, class attendees create magnificent works of glass art, many of which are sold at several yearly exhibitions or through commissions by local businesses and individuals. ■

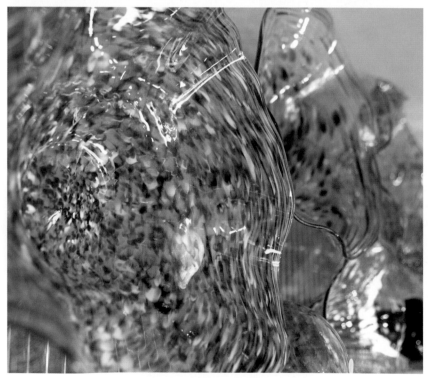

| Photo by **Jim Bryant** |

| Photo by **Jim Bryant** |

Chalkboards are about to become a thing of the past in Tacoma's Fern Hill Elementary School. By utilizing the latest in Smart Board technology, the school's teachers can now project their lesson plans directly off the Internet or their computers and right onto the board's surface—which can also be drawn on and erased just like any other board. "This allows us to open up a whole new world of learning to our students," says Fern Hill's principal, Mario Marsillo. "And we're finding that we're engaging the attention of so many more students this way." Students can also view what's on the board from monitors located at their own desks or in the school's technology lab. Moreover, hooked up to microphones with portable headsets, teachers are able to project more clearly to students who are hearing impaired. ■

| Photo by **Jim Bryant** |

| Photo by **Eric Francis** |

When it comes to academic standards, Tacoma Community College ranks among the top community colleges in the nation. Students Jay Parales and John Rolon are up to the challenge, as they study between classes at the college's Opgaard Student Center.

Tacoma Community College Brings Real-World Focus to Learning

Excellence. Innovation. Diversity. These are the touchstones of Tacoma Community College, and they illustrate the college's commitment to Tacoma and Pierce County. "We pride ourselves on high-quality instruction, focused on effective learning," explains Dr. Pamela J. Transue, TCC president.

Transue is not alone in her assessment: TCC recently ranked as one of the nation's top-performing colleges in the Community College Survey of Student Engagement, a study sponsored by the University of Texas at Austin.

Located in the heart of Tacoma, the college's 150-acre main campus offers academic and occupational degrees, continuing education classes, and developmental learning opportunities. Almost seventeen thousand individuals enroll each year.

TCC traces its roots to 1962, when residents of Tacoma and Pierce County elected to fund a local community college. The college opened for classes on September 28, 1965. Today, 75 percent of TCC students stay in the region and contribute to the local economy after they leave the college.

> *TCC offers academic and occupational degrees, continuing education, and customized training for business and industry.*

Dedicated faculty and staff, specialized counseling, and an accessible campus work to ensure success for students of all ages and backgrounds, and to create a powerful learning environment that includes face-to-face encounters with a variety of cultures and learning styles. More than two hundred international students attend the college each quarter.

The college offers more than forty study areas and sixty professional and technical degrees and certificates. Specialized certificate programs and customized training solutions for business and industry bring a real-world focus to learning. ∎

When two dozen tall ships, with full sails and towering masts, enter the Thea Foss Waterway it's quite a sight. Even more thrilling is the chance to board and tour one of the vessels. In 2005 Tacoma hosted a Tall Ship festival that easily became a captain's favorite. In fact, the American Sail Association bestowed their Port of the Year award on Tacoma for the 2005 festival. Each year the tall ships return to delight mariners and those who just appreciate the grandeur and history of these stately vessels. ■

Goodwill contract employees label soup canisters for Captive Plastics before distribution. Captive Plastics is one of more than twenty businesses that rely on Goodwill for packaging and assembly services, provided on-site at Goodwill's facilities in Tacoma.

| Photo by **Eric Francis** |

Goodwill's "new look" interiors reflect more of a department-store feel. Revenue from retail stores supports job training programs.

Goodwill Changes Lives with Employment Opportunities

Goodwill changes lives by helping people with disabilities or disadvantages go to work. To most people, the name Goodwill conjures up the thought of thrift stores and bargains, and while Tacoma Goodwill Industries does operate twenty retail stores, including seven in Pierce County, it also uniquely combines store values with job training programs that make a difference.

Founded in 1921, Tacoma Goodwill Industries is a not-for-profit organization and is governed by a volunteer board of directors. It's affiliated with Goodwill Industries International and stands as the largest Goodwill in the state of Washington.

The retail side of Goodwill is just the beginning. Tacoma Goodwill accepts donations of gently used clothing, furniture, and household items; sells them at reasonable prices; and puts the revenues into programs that educate, train, and employ people with disabilities or disadvantages.

Programs change lives by helping people with disabilities move into the workforce; they help low-income residents and others needing work skills; and they provide at-risk youth with vital career and educational support.

Goodwill's role in local industry also changes lives through employment. Specialized services such as a car detail shop and a commercial custodial business provide job opportunities. A contracts division provides outsourcing in the areas of assembly, packaging, sorting, shrink-wrapping, bonding, and palletizing to over twenty local and national companies. These commercial services, combined with retail stores, help fund Goodwill programs and provide jobs for approximately 950 people, half of whom have disabilities or disadvantages.

Through job-ready skills and preparation, program participants are able to find employment, so they can support themselves and their families. For Goodwill, training and education are at the center of change. Goodwill's Workforce Development department offers opportunities to learn computer, custodial, clerical, and retail skills; job placement assistance is also offered once training is complete. An adaptive computer lab boasts computers that are specially equipped to meet the needs of those who are sight-impaired or have other physical challenges. A team of staff members and volunteers works alongside participants as they learn job skills or software programs that are in demand throughout today's job market.

The STEPS program helps at-risk youth ages sixteen through twenty-one set goals for their future and prepare for success. STEPS case managers provide one-on-one support and offer both professional development and job opportunities for youth who need help.

If needed, trainers often work side-by-side with a hired program participant, to teach them the on-the-job skills needed to be successful, thus eliminating recruitment and training expenses for the employer, while placing dedicated employees. Within the community, Goodwill builds important relationships so job developers can help program participants secure gainful employment in a variety of fields. More than 150 local companies hire graduates of Goodwill job training programs.

Goodwill is helping people change their lives through employment. For some, a job means a welcome end to welfare or homelessness. For others, it means independence and the ability to successfully provide for themselves and their families. But for all, a job is the key to a new life. This is the heart of Goodwill's mission. ■

One of the ways Tacoma Goodwill Industries changes lives is through providing programs to allow people to learn vital job skills. Here, participants learn the latest computer programs using adaptive technology, such as voice recognition software, in a computer lab funded by a grant from the Bill & Melinda Gates Foundation. Goodwill also makes a second computer lab available to the public for job search assistance.

| Photo by **Eric Francis** |

| Photo by **Jim Bryant** |

| Photo by **Jim Bryant** |

E ach February, patriotism takes center ice when more than ninety local figure skaters of all ages converge at the Sprinker Recreation Center Ice Arena for *Reflections on Ice: America the Beautiful*. During five family-friendly performances presented by the Lakewood Winter Club and Pierce County Parks and Recreation, the cast of skaters, including former world professional champion, renowned choreographer, and Sprinker Recreation Center staff member Lori Benton, presents a spectacular skating extravaganza swathed in red, white, and blue, complete with rousing music, ornate costumes, dazzling athleticism, and a lot of heart. Every year, the show also features special guests, such as world professional pairs champions Elena Leonova and Andrei Khvalko (shown below right). The show, which premiered in 1998, is one of the most anticipated events at the multipurpose, 74,500-square-foot Sprinker Recreation Center, which also boasts the popular Learn to Skate program at the regulation ice arena, as well as indoor and outdoor tennis courts, racquetball and handball courts, softball fields, a baseball field, an all-weather one-quarter-mile track, batting cages, classrooms, a fully equipped pottery room, and much more. The Center is named for Harry H. Sprinker, who served on the county commission for twenty-two years and who established Pierce County's first parks and recreation department. ■

| Photo by **Jim Bryant** |

| Photo by **Brian Dal Balcon**

Throughout the past several years, UWT has received many awards for its innovative work re-adapting Tacoma's historic warehouses and other buildings for instructional use. One such building is the finely restored campus library, built in 1902 as the Snoqualmie Falls Power Company Transformer House.

UW Tacoma Sparks Urban Renewal, Access to Knowledge

More than one hundred years ago, Tacoma's historic Union Station Warehouse District held the raw materials critical to a booming economy as grand brick warehouses with Italian Renaissance features sprang up to serve the terminus of the great transcontinental railroad. Today, these buildings are revitalized to hold goods and services of another kind, most notably the intellectual capital provided by the University of Washington, Tacoma.

Established in 1990 to serve the South Puget Sound region, UWT has developed into a model metropolitan university. While increasing access to bachelor's and master's degrees throughout the South Sound region and expanding boundaries of knowledge and discovery, UWT has also helped enhance the region's business, social, and cultural climate.

A campus of the University of Washington, one of the world's leading research universities, UWT graduates over 850 students a year. Its programs are enriched by students of diverse ages and backgrounds and by a faculty committed not only to high-quality instruction, but also to community engagement and research focused on regional issues. Currently the majority of UWT students are transfers from community colleges, but in fall 2006, UWT will transition to a four-year institution and enroll its first freshman class.

Faculty, staff, and students share expertise by engaging with community agencies, organizations, and businesses.

Since its founding, UWT has provided a world-class education in a small-campus setting. Students become part of a small, vibrant community of enthusiastic learners and critical thinkers who respect diversity and value knowledge. Personalized instruction is a hallmark of the UWT experience.

UWT has also remained committed to engaging the community in mutually beneficial partnerships. It's common for faculty to focus their research on regional issues or problems. Faculty, staff, and students share expertise by engaging with community agencies, organizations, and businesses.

UWT's community connections are also evident in its successful campaigns to establish scholarships and specialized funds to spur campus growth. The regional business community and local governments contributed funds to encourage state lawmakers to establish UWT's Institute of Technology. Established in 2001 to increase the number of Washington residents with bachelor's and master's degrees in high-tech fields, the Institute's programs are attracting related businesses to the area. A $15 million gift in 2003 from the Milgard family of Tacoma expanded the university's Business Administration Program. Now called the Milgard School of Business, it is rapidly gaining a reputation for innovative teaching, a high level of scholarship, and proactive services to the region's business and academic communities.

UW Tacoma is widely credited with fueling urban revitalization in Tacoma by transforming historic buildings into modern university space in the heart of what's become a thriving university and museum district. UWT was recognized by the Sierra Club as one of the nation's best development projects, as well as by the U.S. Green Building Council, National Trust for Historic Preservation, and American Institute of Architects.

When the University of Washington, Tacoma first opened, its goals were to expand South Puget Sound's access to higher education and economic growth. Today it is clear UWT is not only meeting those goals, but exceeding them by leaps and bounds. ■

Built in 1891 as a wholesale dry goods store, the Garretson Woodruff Pratt Building now holds classrooms, a bookstore, and administrative and faculty offices. Seen through the window are Mount Rainier, the Museum of Glass, and the Washington State History Museum. Not only is UWT a beautiful and historic campus, its location provides students with easy access to some of the city's best natural, social, cultural, and employment options.

| Photo by **Eric Francis** |

When it comes to Point Defiance, there's really nothing city about this stunning city park. With 698 acres of dense natural forest, saltwater beaches, breathtaking gardens, hiking and running trails, and much more, Point Defiance Park provides more than 2 million annual visitors with a perfect escape from the bustling city streets that are synonymous with metropolitan life. The park actually was founded in 1841 by Charles Wilkes and eventually was set aside as a military reservation by President Andrew Johnson. However, by 1888, when the area failed to be used for defense purposes, President Grover Cleveland signed legislation allowing the City of Tacoma to develop the land as a public park. In 1905, President Theodore Roosevelt officially awarded ownership of the park to Tacoma. Over the years, the number of maintained acres has grown to more than one hundred. Now, the park features a five-mile drive through an old growth forest, Owen Beach, the Boathouse Marina, numerous gardens cared for by Metro Parks, the Japanese Garden's famous Pagoda that is a replica of a seventeenth-century Japanese Lodge, and the Point Defiance Zoo & Aquarium, a Twenty-nine-acre tourist destination and research facility that boasts an animal collection started in 1891. ■

Point Defiance Park covers 698 acres at the north end of Tacoma. This peninsula into Puget Sound is adjacent to the City of Ruston and has been evolving over the past hundred years in response to the needs of the area. In 1964 the Japanese Garden was built next to the pagoda, which has gone through many changes over the years. It was completed in 1914 as a streetcar station, it became a bus waiting area in 1938, was remodeled in 1963 as a center for flower shows and social gatherings, and in 1988, along with the lodge—the oldest standing structure originally built in the park—it was refurbished and is now a popular rental space for meetings, receptions, and weddings. The Point and its amenities continue to provide city residents, surrounding communities, and national and international visitors a place to touch the water, walk through old-growth forest, and enjoy a variety of events. ∎

An employee of the Solid Waste Division checks the temperature of yard waste—a critical factor in the process of converting yard waste to compost for sale to the public. Recycling is key. If county households recycled half their garbage, it would result in enough energy conservation to light and heat eight thousand homes a year.

| Photo by **Eric Francis** |

Quality of Life Is the Number-One Concern in Pierce County

While there are myriad reasons that Tacoma–Pierce County is one of the best areas in the country to live, there's one that is not so obvious: superior public services.

Pierce County Public Works & Utilities takes the responsibility for quality of life seriously, and by so doing, everyone benefits. "If you live or work in Pierce County, Public Works is all about you," says Brian Ziegler, P.E., director, Pierce County Public Works & Utilities. "We do the work, and you get the benefit."

While it's easy to take roads, ferries, and airports—as well as sewers and solid waste management—for granted, the public expects reliable, efficient, responsive service. Imagine how messy life would be without a competent transportation system, for example. The overall efforts of the road traffic engineers and technicians result in better traffic flow, safer roads, and less time waiting at intersections. The division is responsible for monitoring traffic, developing short-term solutions, identifying long-range needs, installing and maintaining traffic control devices, and perhaps most important, ensuring safety. Even something as simple as a missing stop sign puts lives at risk. And because safe roads are the result of well-maintained roads, the Road Maintenance Division diligently maintains all 1,550 miles of Pierce County roads, which includes snow and ice control, as well as efficient response to natural disasters and accidents.

"Look close at any successful community in America, and you'll find a highly skilled, well-run, and innovative public works and utilities department."

Traffic on some of the area's major roadways is expected to double in the coming years. The Road Planning and Programming Division is charged with understanding both the current and future transportation needs of the county. By working closely with Pierce County residents, local officials, and other agencies, the division develops long-term transportation needs and mobility strategies. Each year, this data is used to prepare the County's Transportation Improvement Program, which the road project engineers and construction engineers rely on to design and oversee the construction projects to improve safety and solve congestion.

Something as basic and essential as clean water and safe floodplains is another area of the Public Works and Utilities Department that requires continual focus on new techniques and approaches that will improve quality and cost-effectiveness of service. "Because clean water supports healthy habitat and healthy people, Pierce County Water Programs supports clean water," explains Ziegler. "We provide storm drainage systems and maintain the flood control elements of the Puyallup, White, and Carbon rivers. In managing the water that flows into our creeks, rivers, lakes, and estuaries, our responsibilities include flood hazard reduction, water quality, and water-related habitat." Water Programs uses a comprehensive and integrated approach to surface water management for unincorporated Pierce County. Natural systems are used to preserve the creeks, streams, and rivers, ensuring the right balance of clean water for the community and vital habitat for aquatic species. After all, Tacoma and Pierce County are known for their ecological stewardship.

Equally important to the environment, as well as public health, is the proficient collection and treatment of wastewater. Recognized by the Environmental Protection Agency for excellence in operations and maintenance, Pierce County's Chambers Creek Regional Wastewater Treatment Plan is an advanced secondary treatment

| Continued on page 46 |

More than ninety-two miles of levee, and three hundred storm-water ponds like this one, are maintained by the Water Programs Division of Pierce County Public Works & Utilities. The underlying goal is to ensure the delicate balance between flood control, clean water for the community, and a healthy habitat for all.

| Photo by **Eric Francis** |

| Photo by **Eric Francis** |

Pierce County provides new and improved roads to address current congestion and to meet future travel demand. Lake Tapps Parkway, shown here, was a coordinated improvement with many partners to provide a key roadway to connect communities across the county.

|Continued from page 45 |

facility that services more than 165,000 people in approximately fourteen communities. Considering these customers produce enough wastewater daily to fill more than twenty-eight Olympic-sized swimming pools, and the fact that this wastewater must be treated before it can be discharged to the environment, the plant's role in protecting the environment cannot be understated. "We continually look for new ways to reuse byproducts of the treatment process," says Ziegler. "For example, reclaimed wastewater will be treated for future irrigation of the Chambers Creek Properties—the unique set of parcels owned by our department. This land will provide clean, safe areas for public recreation, as well as government use, all the while preserving the shoreline and its surrounding environment."

| Photo by **Eric Francis** |

More than two hundred thousand people utilize the Pierce County ferries every year. Providing a mainland link to Anderson and Ketron islands, the ferries safely transport passengers for work and pleasure. Pierce County Public Works & Utilities is one of the few departments of its kind in the state to manage a ferry system.

A mechanic works on a private aircraft at Pierce County Airport. Purchased by Pierce County in 1979, Thun Field is home to approximately 250 single-engine and multi-engine aircraft. In a single year, more than one hundred thousand takeoffs and landings occur at this facility.

| Photo by **Eric Francis** |

| Photo by **Eric Francis** |

The Pierce County Chambers Creek Regional Wastewater Treatment Plant is recognized by the EPA for Excellence in Operations and Maintenance, as well as the State Department of Ecology for Outstanding Performance. One of the new ways to reuse byproducts of the treatment process includes a system to apply biosolids as a soil enhancer.

Another part of the department that protects and enhances public health and the natural environment is the Solid Waste Division. Through partnering with city and town governments, the division plans and manages efficient waste reduction, recycling, composting, disposal, and household hazardous waste programs, avoiding duplication of services and saving citizens money in the long run.

"Look close at any successful community in America, and you'll find a highly skilled, well-run, and innovative public works and utilities department," says county executive John Ladenburg. "It's certainly true in Pierce County. These professionals are the reason our neighborhoods don't just have good roads; they have an efficient transportation system. They're why our county doesn't just have clean water; it has thriving streams and rivers. They're why our citizens don't just have adequate sewer and solid waste services; they have a healthy environment. No wonder Pierce County has been singled out as one of the most livable counties in the country." ■

| Photo by **Jim Bryant** |

When #23 Marcus Trufant takes his place as cornerback for the Seattle Seahawks, the fun-loving Sea Hawkers know their team is in good hands. That's because this Tacoma native has already built a stellar reputation for defense since being picked by the Seahawks in the first round of the 2003 NFL draft. As a rookie, Trufant started all sixteen games, racking up sixty-nine solo tackles and two interceptions. In his second year with the Seahawks, Trufant became one of only four cornerbacks in league history to lead his team in total tackles, making ninety-three in a single season. His five interceptions for the season also earned him high rankings in both the NFC and NFL. Holding tackling and interception records is nothing new for Trufant; in the last two seasons he played for his college alma mater, Washington State, Trufant did not allow a single touchdown reception, and before he graduated from Tacoma's Wilson High School, he had tallied forty-eight tackles and eight interceptions. "Playing in Seattle is a dream come true," says Trufant. "There's nothing better than getting support from the fans you grew up with." ■

| Photo by **Jim Bryant** |

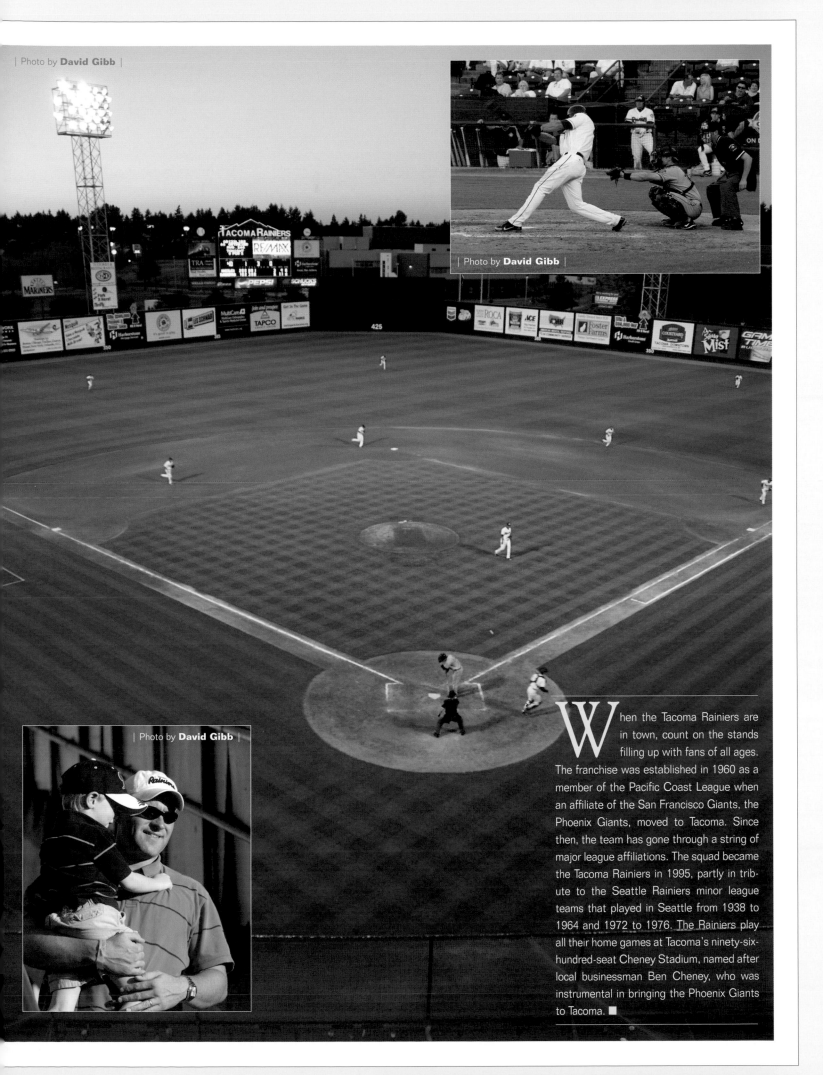

When the Tacoma Rainiers are in town, count on the stands filling up with fans of all ages. The franchise was established in 1960 as a member of the Pacific Coast League when an affiliate of the San Francisco Giants, the Phoenix Giants, moved to Tacoma. Since then, the team has gone through a string of major league affiliations. The squad became the Tacoma Rainiers in 1995, partly in tribute to the Seattle Rainiers minor league teams that played in Seattle from 1938 to 1964 and 1972 to 1976. The Rainiers play all their home games at Tacoma's ninety-six-hundred-seat Cheney Stadium, named after local businessman Ben Cheney, who was instrumental in bringing the Phoenix Giants to Tacoma. ■

| Photo by **Eric Francis** |

Since 1946, Cascade Regional Blood Services has been a resource for hospitals and trauma centers in the South Puget Sound area. Cascade is a volunteer-supported, not-for-profit organization. The forty-foot bloodmobile was completely underwritten by community supporters. These bloodmobiles are a familiar sight at businesses, churches, schools, and civic organizations. The happy faces of the cartoon kids decorating the vehicle represent lives saved by blood donors.

| Photo by **Eric Francis** |

Giving Blood Is a Precious Gift—The Gift of Life

Ninety-five percent of the population may need a blood transfusion within their lifetime—a significant fact when you realize that only 5 percent of the eligible population donates blood.

"A blood donor is a special kind of volunteer," said Kelley Gregory, marketing manager at Cascade Regional Blood Services. "They donate a gift more precious than time or money: the gift of life. Each donation can help save the life of a family member, a friend, or neighbor, right here in our community."

Since 1946 Cascade Regional Blood Services has served hospitals in the South Puget Sound area as an independent, volunteer-supported, not-for-profit community blood center. These hospitals include Mary Bridge Children's Hospital, Tacoma General, St. Joseph Medical Center, Good Samaritan, St. Clare, St. Francis, and Allenmoore Hospital.

> *"Each donation can help save the life of a family member, a friend, or neighbor, right here in our community."*

There is a constant need for blood, because it has a limited shelf life and because the South Puget Sound area has many sophisticated medical facilities where patients require blood for normal everyday procedures, emergency surgeries, and life-threatening treatments. "There are eight different blood types and several components to consider, so it is an ongoing challenge to meet the specific daily needs of each hospital," Gregory explained.

Cascade Regional Blood Services regularly conducts blood drives at area organizations, churches, malls, schools, and special events in order to make donating more convenient. In addition, Cascade maintains offices in Tacoma, Puyallup, and Federal Way. "We also have a solid base of committed frequent donors who make our mission part of their mission. So if you have ever wondered if your donation is needed, the answer is yes, absolutely." ■

| Photo by **Alan S. Weiner** |

August 2006 marked the tenth anniversary of the relocation of the Washington State History Museum to its new home at Pacific Avenue, the first step in establishing downtown Tacoma's new cultural district. Today, the building's dramatic arches are one of many architectural landmarks in the district, which also include the city's historic Union Station, the Tacoma Art Museum, and the Museum of Glass, with its spectacular pedestrian walkway (shown right). With a mission to preserve and disseminate the history of the Pacific Northwest, the 106,000-square-foot Washington State History Museum hosts juried art shows, special events, workshops, and temporary exhibits that cover everything from the Lewis and Clark expedition to the state's battle against tuberculosis to a photographic history of the Columbia River. Permanent exhibits include the Great Wall of Washington History, an 1,800-square-foot model railroad, and an interactive history lab that teaches students and teachers how to apply the basic concepts of historical study. ■

| Photo by **Jackson Hill** |

Milgard's legendary commitment to field service extends a full lifetime warranty covering all materials and labor for as long as original homeowners reside in their home.

Milgard Manufacturing Is Unmatched in Quality and Service

In 1958, Gary Milgard helped found the Milgard Glass Company with his father in a small building in Tacoma. Gary's brother Jim joined the glass company in 1961. In 1962, Gary started a new aluminum window fabricating company, Milgard Manufacturing, with the goal of providing the most reliable source of quality aluminum windows and patio doors in the industry. Milgard's original commitment to quality and service has continued to be key to the company's success.

Today, Milgard employs approximately twenty-three hundred people in the Tacoma area. Milgard now offers a full line of aluminum, vinyl, and fiberglass windows and patio doors. In fact, Milgard has been recognized for manufacturing the nation's highest-quality vinyl windows six of the last eight years in a yearly independent survey sponsored by Hanley-Wood, Inc., publishers of *BUILDER* magazine. Milgard windows are guaranteed for as long as the original homeowner owns the home, covering all materials and labor.

Each home has a personality, and Milgard has the right windows and doors to enhance that unique character perfectly. No other company can match Milgard's product breadth, innovation, or passion for customer service. Every

---

Each home has a personality, and Milgard has the right windows and doors to enhance that unique character perfectly.

---

window and door is custom-built for each order. Given every choice and option, Milgard can create over 4.5 million possible window and door configurations. Milgard controls the entire production, delivery, and service process, keeping quality a priority and lead times to a minimum. As Milgard continues to expand nationally, its focus remains on building one exceptional window or door at a time. Going to market through a network of dedicated dealers, Milgard creates products to help homeowners turn their dreams into reality.

Community support is a mainstay focus at Milgard. Carol Milgard created a program many years ago to address community needs near all Milgard facilities. Known as "MG/CAT," the "MG" stands for Matching Gift, where Milgard will match donations made to the qualified charity of their employees' choosing. The "CAT" refers to "Community Action Team," through which each Milgard location organizes events and projects to serve community needs and underprivileged populations.

Corporate offices in the Fife area oversee nineteen factory locations stretching from coast to coast, with more than five thousand employees nationwide. In 2001, Masco Corporation purchased Milgard. Headquartered in Taylor, Michigan, Masco is one of the world's largest manufacturers of brand-name consumer products for the home and family. ∎

Milgard Windows operates a state-of-the-art vinyl window and patio door manufacturing facility in Fife, Washington, along with additional plants in the area that produce vinyl frames, fiberglass frames, tempered glass, and fiberglass windows and patio doors.

| Photo by **Jackson Hill** |

W ithout a doubt, one of the best ways to fully experience the natural beauty that surrounds Tacoma is from the seat of a bicycle. And one of the best reasons to hop on a two-wheeler is the Daffodil Classic, the highly anticipated annual road tour organized by the Tacoma Wheelman's Bicycle Club, an organization founded in 1888 to promote "safe bicycling for recreation, health, and alternate transportation." The event, which has taken place during the Daffodil Festival each spring since the mid-1970s, gives both cycling enthusiasts and novices the chance to get out and put the pedal to the pavement for an extremely pleasurable ride through rural Pierce County. Participants can choose to follow a twenty-, fifty-, seventy-, or one-hundred-mile course during the ride. The collective route actually comprises two major fifty-mile loops that take riders through some of the most splendid terrain found in the Northwest, from natural rivers and lakes to scenic forestland. "There are many beautiful views, but some of the most memorable are of Mount Rainier, which is visible from many locations," says Tim Payne, president of the Tacoma Wheelman's Bicycle Club. "And the locations can actually make it look quite different depending on where you are." In recent years, the club has added a twenty-mile fun ride that allows families to explore the local foothills on paved off-roads that run along a fairly flat railroad grade, which is perfect for smaller children to traverse. Depending on the weather each year, the road tour, which begins and ends in Orting, can attract as many as twenty-two hundred riders, who are all treated to a truly unique adventure. ■

| Photo by **Alan S. Weiner** |

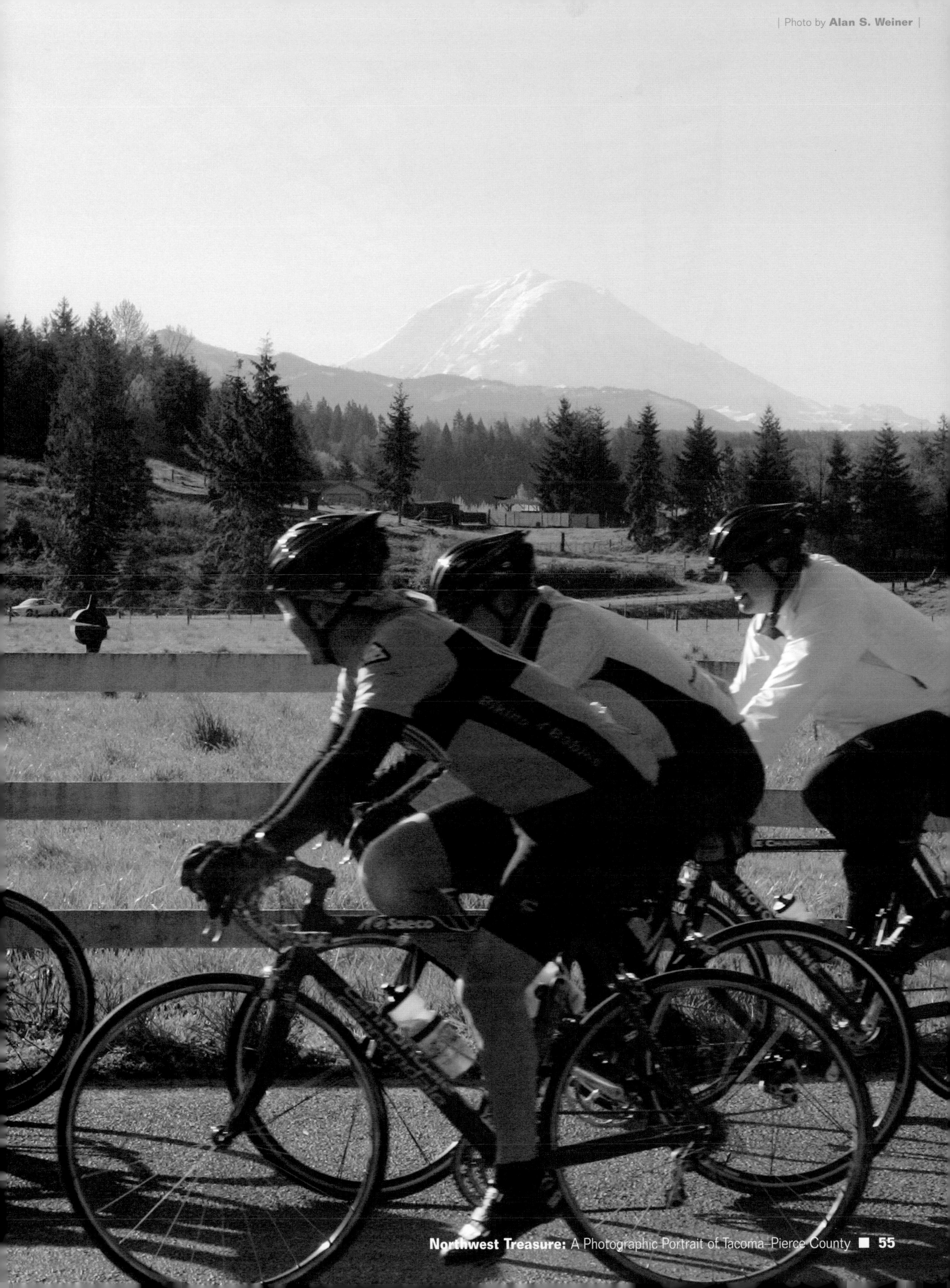

| Photo by **Jackson Hill** |

Wells Fargo–Serving the Puget Sound Region since 1857

The name "Wells Fargo" is forever linked with the image of a six-horse stagecoach thundering across the American West loaded with gold. Just five years after the company was founded in 1852, it opened agencies in logging towns on the Puget Sound. Today across Washington, Wells Fargo has 151 banking stores, including 10 locations in Pierce County.

Wells Fargo's Community Banking approach means that all decisions are made locally, on behalf of the customers, businesses, and communities they serve. This approach applies to all Wells Fargo products and services, including consumer and business banking, mortgages, investments, insurance, commercial banking, and home equity lending.

Wells Fargo's Community Banking approach means that all decisions are made locally, on behalf of the customers, businesses, and communities they serve.

One of Wells Fargo's most important strategies is to "out-local the nationals and out-national the locals," meaning that Wells Fargo is determined to outperform large national banks by never wavering from their community-banking and local decision-making approach to delivering financial services. It also means that Wells Fargo is determined to outperform the local, smaller banks by being more innovative, offering more products and services, and having more resources to identify and develop today what customers will want and need tomorrow.

Wells Fargo recently provided grants to 325 Washington nonprofit organizations, giving more than $2.2 million in funds, educational matching gifts, and in-kind gifts.

Now, more than 150 years after the 1852 Gold Rush, Wells Fargo still maintains the reputation of trust by dealing rapidly and responsibly to meet all of our customers' financial needs. ■

With evergreens framing the greens and even a majestic fir tree in the middle of the seventh fairway, Lake Spanaway in Pierce County is the epitome of a great Northwest golf course, where the natural charm of the region simply adds to the playability. Lake Spanaway has the distinction of being the last course designed by nationally renowned golf course architect A. Vernon Macan. Recent renovations on this classic layout have made it even more enjoyable for the everyday golfer, with tees ranging from fifty-six hundred to seven thousand yards. However, the course remains challenging enough for more expert golfers and regularly hosts championships, including the Annual Puget Sound Amateur. ■

| Photo by **David Gibb** |

| Photo by **David Gibb** |

| Photo by **David Gibb** |

The distinctive neighborhoods of Tacoma, as much as anything else, give the city its charm and vitality. Take Old Town or the Historic Proctor District, for instance. Old Town was founded by pioneer Job Carr. Just a block inland from Commencement Bay is North Thirtieth Street, which features ornamental streetlights and turn-of-the century buildings. Sitting in a small park below hills lined with beautiful homes is the recently opened Job Carr Cabin Museum. The original cedar-log cabin served as Tacoma's first post office. Shops and cafes are springing up, and visitors are coming to look and to enjoy the atmosphere. For residents, the Proctor District is a charming small town in the heart of a large city. Located just to the north of the University of Puget Sound, houses in the neighborhood range from new construction to stately old homes that have been standing for more than a century. In a short, three-block stroll you can find a gift store, bookstore, toy store, apparel store, hobby store, bank, health club, beauty shop, post office, library, elementary school, middle school, and a church. There are also several bed-and-breakfasts, thirteen restaurants, and one of the country's longest-operating movie theaters. ■

TACOMA DOME STATION

Some cities are close to being pedestrian-perfect. Tacoma, with its friendly Dome District brimming with activities in its mini-neighborhoods, is one of them. From myriad museums to one-of-a-kind restaurants and shops, the area captivates the curious and entertains all. Anchoring the district, the 6.1-acre Tacoma Dome Entertainment Complex is often a central attraction, as its technological features continue to provide optimal audio and visual for the myriad events held there since opening in 1983. The dome's size is hard to miss, and the exterior's blue and white pattern intentionally mirrors the great Northwest's beautiful waters and mountains. And, when pedestrians want a swift trip to other venues in the districts, pedestrians can take a load off their feet and ride the Tacoma Link—an efficient light-rail line with stations conveniently positioned throughout the downtown core. ◼

The Dome District

DaVita, Inc. is located in the historic Peter Sandberg Building in downtown Tacoma. Originally built in 1907 and restored for DaVita by Horizon Partners NW in 1999, it is home to the kidney dialysis company's business office.

| Photo by **Jackson Hill** |

DaVita, Inc. Offers Compassion and Convenience to Its Patients

For patients diagnosed with chronic kidney disease (CKD), the notion of enduring regular dialysis treatments can be a daunting one. However, in Tacoma–Pierce County, local residents who need this vital, lifesaving treatment can turn to DaVita, Inc., the country's leading independent provider of dialysis services. With three centers in Lakewood, Puyallup, and Tacoma, as well as one in Federal Way in neighboring South King County, DaVita gives patients convenient access to professional and compassionate care in a warm and welcoming environment.

DaVita, Inc. is actually an El Segundo, California–based company that serves over 94,500 patients nationwide each year with more than twelve hundred outpatient dialysis centers in forty-one states and the District of Columbia and inpatient dialysis services in over three hundred hospitals. While corporate operations have been headquartered in the Golden State since a 1995 leveraged buyout from National Medical Enterprises, Inc., allowed DaVita to begin operating independently, Tacoma is home to the company's main business office. This presence, along with the four local dialysis centers, has made DaVita one of the area's most valuable resources in more ways than one.

From a patient's perspective, DaVita is a much-needed respite from the archetypal hospital experience, offering a calming locale where he or she can receive comprehensive treatment from highly trained technicians, nurses, dietitians, and social workers. "Our patients' health and well-being are our first priority," explains Kristin Videto, facilities manager. "We care about them, and we do all we can to make sure they get the best care possible."

From a patient's perspective, DaVita is a much-needed respite from the archetypal hospital experience, offering a calming locale where he or she can receive comprehensive treatment.

In fact, the word "DaVita" derives from an Italian phrase meaning "he/she gives life," and all of the company's employees, or teammates, take this responsibility seriously, understanding the impact they have on their patients. For this reason, teammates strictly adhere to DaVita's seven core values: service excellence, integrity, team, continuous improvement, accountability, fulfillment, and fun.

These principles relate directly to the company's mission, which is to be "the provider, partner, and employer of choice." In Tacoma, DaVita certainly has fulfilled this goal. Not only have numerous local nephrologists partnered with the company to help countless patients obtain its exceptional services, but DaVita also is the tenth-largest employer in the area. Fifty teammates staff the dialysis centers, while the business office, which is located in the historic 1907 Peter Sandberg Building and handles the entire company's payroll, accounts payable, and bookkeeping, employs over seven hundred people.

Additionally, the company has committed itself to strengthening the local community by sponsoring the PC Juvenile Diabetes Walk, serving as a Top 25 supporter of the local United Way, and more. DaVita also is involved in grassroots letter-writing campaigns through its DaVita Patient Citizens Group, a body that helps educate political leaders about CKD patients and how they benefit from the services independent providers like DaVita offer.

Ultimately, DaVita would like to be known as "the greatest dialysis company the world has ever seen." From its success thus far, in Tacoma and nationwide, it appears that the company is on target to achieve its dream. ■

DaVita, Inc.'s Tacoma Dialysis Center offers state-of-the-art equipment as part of its mission to be the provider, partner, and employer of choice. The facility is located near Allenmore Hospital in Tacoma.

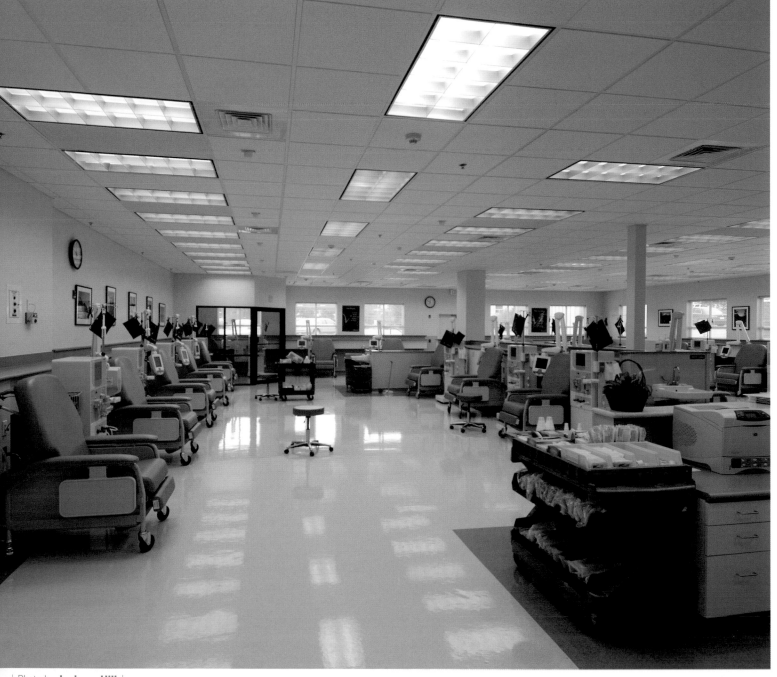

| Photo by **Jackson Hill** |

Do the Puyallup!

September just isn't September without the thrills of the annual Puyallup Fair. Hold on to your hat and let it all out. This ride's name says it all. Extreme Scream is a crowd favorite, as each year tens of thousands of brave thrill riders get a chance to stretch their vocal cords. A fair just isn't a fair without trying to win a great prize like this oversized but cuddly stuffed animal. Every year about 1.3 million people seek out the games, the rides, the exhibits, and the traditional tastes offered over the seventeen days that the fair runs. As a result, the Puyallup Fair and Events Center brings more than $200 million to the city, county, and state. ■

| Photo by **Jim Bryant** |

THE PARATROOPER

#*32101

Lots of things in this world are changing, but it's nice to know you can still count on some things. The Pierce County Fair is one of them. After more than sixty years, folks still congregate in Graham, Washington, for a four-day celebration of rural life, agriculture, and "good ol' fashioned values." The name has changed from the 4-H Fair, and the location has changed from the days when it was held in Benson Grange, but according to the organizers, "The goals and functions of the fair did not change. It still serves the youth of Pierce County." The fair is made possible through the efforts of hundreds of volunteers, as well as the cooperation of the Pierce County Fair Association and Pierce County Parks and Recreation. From the Puyallup Rotarian's sponsored pancake breakfast for exhibitors and superintendents, the judging of home economic and livestock competitions, the carnival rides, the food, and the free entertainment, to the naming of the Royal Court, tradition holds sway. Folks come from miles around to eat, to play, to enjoy some friendly competition, maybe to go home with a blue ribbon, but always to go home with happy memories and anticipation of next year's fair. ■

| Photo by **Jim Bryant** |

The Boeing Frederickson plant serves as a major supplier of wing components and empennage structures to Boeing Commercial Airplanes. Established in 1992, Boeing Frederickson is located in unincorporated Pierce County southeast of Tacoma and is the youngest major manufacturing operation in Boeing Commercial Airplanes. Approximately twelve hundred people work at the site, including support and production employees.

Boeing: A Leader in Aerospace and in Community Service

In 1908 a man with a special interest in airplanes moved to Seattle. It took him eight years to incorporate his airplane manufacturing business as Pacific Aero Products Company, but he persevered. The man was William Boeing, and today the high-tech company that bears his name is known all over the world. Closer to home, Boeing is the largest private employer in Washington, and Tacoma is the headquarters of its Commercial Airplanes business unit.

Currently Boeing has customers in 145 countries and supplies roughly 75 percent of the world's commercial jetliners. However, even with those impressive numbers, developing and maintaining healthy communities is so important to Boeing that it is part of the company's mission. "We believe in good corporate citizenship. We will provide a safe workplace and protect the environment. We will promote the health and well-being of Boeing people and their families. We will work with our communities by volunteering and financially supporting education and other worthy causes."

Although the Boeing presence is familiar in Tacoma, the public may not be as familiar with the specifics of the company's operations. Here is a closer look at the world's leading aerospace company.

Boeing provides end-to-end services for large-scale systems that combine sophisticated communication networks with air, land, sea, and space-based platforms for global military, government, and commercial customers.

> *Developing and maintaining healthy communities is so important to Boeing that it is part of the company's mission.*

It arranges, structures, and provides financing to facilitate the sale and delivery of satellites and launch vehicles, as well as commercial and military aircraft. By providing high-speed, two-way connectivity in its planes, it is possible for in-flight passengers and crew to use secure, high-speed access for the Internet, personal and business email accounts, and company intranets.

Three other business units complete the picture: Boeing Integrated Defense Systems, Connexion by Boeing℠, and Boeing Capital Corporation. Supporting these units is the Shared Services Group, which provides a broad range of services to Boeing worldwide, and Boeing Technology-Phantom Works, which helps develop, acquire, apply, and protect innovative technologies and processes.

Another important element is the Boeing Frederickson plant, established in 1992 and located in unincorporated Pierce County. It is the youngest major manufacturing operation in Commercial Airplanes and a major supplier of wing components and empennage structures for the business unit. Approximately twelve hundred people work at the site, including support and production employees.

Wherever Boeing has facilities, the company focuses giving on education, health and human services, culture and the arts, and civic and environmental issues, investing more than $20 million to the Puget Sound community each year. Employees—both present and retired—are also encouraged to get involved. For example, in 2005 employees donated more than $19.5 million, including approximately twenty-three thousand books, more than six thousand backpacks, and three hundred tote boxes of school supplies to less-advantaged Puget Sound students.

When they hear the name "Boeing," many people will think of the Space Shuttle or the 787 Dreamliner, a super-efficient airplane expected to be in service in 2008, but that is only part of the story of this company and the more than sixty-two thousand employees in the Puget Sound region. ■

Boeing employee Phil Lathrop inspects vacuum fittings inside a huge autoclave, thirty feet in diameter, which is used to slow bake, or cure, composite parts at the Boeing Frederickson Composite Manufacturing Center (CMC). The composite parts are assembled into what's called the empennage—load-bearing primary structures that stabilize an airplane in flight. In addition to building the composite "tail" of the Boeing 777, the CMC also serves as a major structures partner to the Boeing 787 Dreamliner to provide a fully functioning vertical fin.

A Sense of Pride

On October 27, 2005, the First Brigade, Twenty-fifth Infantry Division, Stryker Brigade Combat Team received a much-deserved hero's welcome during its redeployment ceremony at Fort Lewis. The team spent one year serving on the front lines in Iraq, from September 2004 to October 2005, training Iraqi soldiers, helping form police units, building roads, opening schools, and making the American people back at home proud. During the tour, the brigade lost thirty-three Strykers, who were honored during the ceremony; it also saw more than six hundred wounded, with each injured soldier receiving the Purple Heart upon his or her return. The redeployment ceremony, which included the uncasing of the brigade's colors to signify its completed mission, led the day of family fun, which culminated in a barbecue and huge shindig held in a hangar at neighboring Gray Army Air Field. The event, complete with live music and copious amounts of food, gave attendees like Cathy Bachl and her daughter Lily the chance to spend some highly anticipated time with their loved ones after a lengthy separation. After the ceremony and celebration, the returning soldiers looked forward to some well-earned R&R and the chance to get back to normal life for a while. ■

Many residential homes in Tacoma are representative of traditional Northwest coastal architecture, which includes the use of cedar shingles and large, multipaned windows. Some of them are beautifully restored and maintained historic homes, some of them meticulous reproductions. But all reflect a pride of ownership in their distinctive styling.

Tudor-Gothic architecture blends with groves of fir trees that wind through the campus.

| Photo by **Ross Mulhausen** | © University of Puget Sound

University of Puget Sound Cultivates Leaders for the Future

In 1888—a full year before Washington achieved statehood—the University of Puget Sound was founded as an institution of education, inspiration, and promise. Today, some of the nation's brightest and most accomplished students come from forty-seven states and thirteen countries to engage in a liberal arts education that prepares them for lives of leadership and service.

At the core of Puget Sound's educational vision is developing the ability to think independently, logically, and analytically. "Our role is to be a cauldron for leadership," says president Ronald R. Thomas, "a laboratory in which to create and test ideas, to discover and expand knowledge, to critique and transform our culture."

A low student-faculty ratio provides Puget Sound students with personal attention from faculty who have a strong commitment to teaching and represent a diverse range of scholars, experts, and researchers from around the globe. More than two hundred faculty members offer twelve hundred courses each year in more than forty major fields. Distinctive academic opportunities include a conservatory-quality School of Music, a School of Business and Leadership, and a variety of international and interdisciplinary programs. Puget Sound is also the only nationally ranked independent undergraduate liberal arts college in western Washington, and one of just five independent colleges in the Northwest granted a charter by Phi Beta Kappa, the nation's most prestigious academic honor society.

A unique intellectual asset in our region and in the nation, University of Puget Sound offers an education steeped in the liberal arts.

"The university is a unique intellectual asset in our region and in the nation," explains Thomas, "offering an integrated and collaborative education steeped in the liberal arts and committed to being environmentally responsible, civically engaged, and globally aware."

That awareness starts close to home. Approximately three-quarters of the student body are involved in service activities throughout Pierce County, ranging from participation in the university's Civic Scholarship Initiative (in which students work closely with faculty on research projects of local and national significance) to mentoring local schoolchildren and distributing food to homeless shelters. With the signing of the Talloires Declaration in 2005,

University of Puget Sound joined institutions of higher learning around the world in a commitment to environmental sustainability. Students' commitments to service extend far beyond graduation; the university has consistently ranked among the top five American small colleges with the most alumni currently volunteering in the Peace Corps. In addition, the Tacoma Art Museum, the Tacoma Actor's Guild, and the Tacoma Symphony Orchestra all trace their origins to students and faculty from the university.

Each fall, nearly twenty-six hundred students converge on Puget Sound's beautiful Tudor-Gothic campus in Tacoma's historic North End. Seventy-five percent of those students come from outside Washington state, and many remain in the area after graduation, fueling Tacoma's economic and cultural renaissance. Puget Sound graduates include Rhodes and Fulbright scholars, notables in the arts and culture, entrepreneurs and elected officials, and leaders in business and finance locally and throughout the world.

"Here at the University of Puget Sound," says Thomas, "we seek to cultivate the leaders of the next generation. They are the ones in whom we invest our hope to secure our future." ■

Nearby Point Defiance and Commencement Bay provide students and professors with numerous opportunities for scientific study and field research.

Photo by **Ross Mulhausen** | © University of Puget Sound

The Tacoma Art Museum opened its new facility in 2003 in the heart of the Cultural District, the final stop on a journey that began in 1935 and included five other locations over the years. "Our mission is to connect people and art, and one of the ways we do that is by holding classes throughout the year," said Kristy Gledhill, director of communications. "Sometimes the students make 'Chihulies' out of cellophane, and around the holidays we had a fused-glass class conducted by Northwest glass artist Cindy Miller." More than 60 percent of the museum's exhibit space is committed to the work of artists in the Northwest. To encourage visitors to create their own works of art inspired by the exhibits, there is an Open Art Center complete with volunteers and suitcases containing different kinds of arts supplies, such as watercolors or pastels. Participants can take their artwork home, or leave it to be displayed on the wall. And watching over everything is a giant cardboard sculpture created by Scott Fife and modeled on his dog, Leroy. ∎

Tacoma Public Utilities is accessible and accountable to its customer-owners.

| Photo by **Jackson Hill** |

Tacoma Public Utilities Offers Around-the-Clock Reliable Service

The flick of a switch. The turn of a tap. The rumble of a freight train. Most of us don't give much thought to these everyday occurrences. Given our advanced technological age, we have rightly come to expect the seamless delivery of reliable power, clean water, and basic goods and services.

Tacoma Public Utilities ensures just that kind of delivery. As one of the oldest and largest municipally owned utilities in the country, it has provided customers throughout Tacoma and much of Pierce County with reliable, high-quality, innovative, and competitively priced services since 1893.

Tacoma Public Utilities is also distinguished by its unique operating structure. A five-member, all-volunteer board provides policy guidance and oversight for three distinct service providers: Tacoma Power, Tacoma Water, and Tacoma Rail. The director of utilities is the chief executive officer; each division is guided by a superintendent and various operations managers.

Innovative and forward-thinking, Tacoma Power is redefining the connection between customer and utility. Certainly, building and updating infrastructure is a major part of the utility's mission. To handle projected growth in the area, five new substations are scheduled to come on line within the next few years, while the utility's 6,244-foot-

> *Innovative and forward-thinking, Tacoma Power is redefining the connection between customer and utility.*

long, single-span transmission line across the Tacoma Narrows will further reduce maintenance costs and increase reliability within the system. A project involving high-tech meters will integrate the utility's telecommunications network with electrical services, which will streamline everything from remote meter reading to load tracking.

Another innovation is Tacoma Power's telecommunications network. Originally planned as a fiber-optic network to improve electric utility operations, management soon realized that the network offered additional benefits. As a result, Tacoma Power created Click! Network to provide customers with choices for cable television, high-speed Internet access, and broadband services. Thanks to innovations like these, more than 165,000 residential, commercial, and industrial customers enjoy the most reliable, low-cost electrical services in all of Puget Sound, plus more choices for telecommunications services.

Innovative thinking also guides Tacoma Water in its mission to protect public health and to provide customers with an abundant supply of water that meets state and federal safety requirements.

The utility just completed a new treatment plant, a major upgrade of intake facilities, and a 34-mile-long pipeline from the Green River watershed into the city of Tacoma.

For over eighty years, Tacoma Water has managed and guarded the quality of water in this watershed, a 148,000-acre collecting point for melting snow and seasonal rainfall located in the Cascade Mountains. As the utility's major water source, Green River supplies customers with up to 78 million gallons of water each day.

| Continued on page 74 |

Tacoma Power provides reliable, low-cost electricity to 165,000 customers in the Tacoma and Pierce County area.

| Photo by **Jackson Hill** |

| Continued from page 73 |

Tacoma Water also owns and maintains twenty-four wells located in and around the city. Because they can supply up to 40 percent of Tacoma Water's water during summer's peak use months, these wells too undergo continuous and rigorous monitoring for water quality and safety.

Tacoma Water leads the way in regional conservation efforts. As a founding member of Partnership for Water Conservation, a group of water utilities, environmental groups, and businesses interested in promoting water conservation, Tacoma Water is committed to a 10 percent reduction in water use by 2010. And through an agreement with the Muckleshoot Indian Tribe and the State of Washington, Tacoma Water is helping restore the Green River as a productive salmon stream.

The utility's third division, Tacoma Rail, supplies Pierce County residents with another vital service. Tacoma Rail was built in the early twentieth century to provide trolley service to the industrial tideflats; after World War II its passenger operations were transferred to the Tacoma Transit Company, and Tacoma Rail retained the freight switching operations.

With three divisions and eighteen diesel locomotives that make over one hundred thousand line hauls per year, Tacoma Rail is one of the largest short-line railroads in the country. It is also a vital component of economic growth in the region. Not only does Tacoma Rail switch freight between Tacoma-based industries and two transcontinental railroads, it also serves one of the largest container ports in North America, the bustling

| Photo by **Eric Francis** |

| Photo by **Jackson Hill** |

Tacoma Water provides pure, reliable water that supports our economy and enhances the quality of life for ninety thousand customers.

Click! Network service technician Andy Aubry confers with customer Sally Perkins before adding the latest technology to her historic home in Tacoma.

The Salvation Army Giving
Tree is just one of Tacoma Public Utilities' many community outreach activities. It is the second-largest giving tree in the area.

| Photo by **Jackson Hill** |

Port of Tacoma. Each year, the Port of Tacoma handles more than 2 million twenty-foot containers from worldwide shipping giants like Evergreen, "K" Line, and Hyundai. Tacoma Rail is the crucial link that efficiently and cost-effectively switches goods between these trans-Pacific cargo ships and trans-American railroads.

By overseeing the operations of three separate divisions, Tacoma Public Utilities plays an important role in helping its customers better their lives, safeguard their families, and grow the businesses that keep Pierce County going strong. ■

Tacoma Rail is a vital link
between shippers, local industries, and our economy.

| Photo by **Eric Francis** |

| Photo by **Alan S. Weiner** |

| Photo by **Sonja Hall** |

Celebrating Community

| Photo by **Alan S. Weiner** |

On September 30, 1889, six weeks before Washington became a state, a group of sail and power boaters decided to form a yachting club. The following year they adopted bylaws that set the initiation fee at seventy-five dollars with annual dues of twenty-five dollars. Thirty-six years later, daffodils came to the Puyallup Valley to replace the area's dying hop industry. The next year Mr. and Mrs. Charles W. Orton opened their home for a garden party to let guests see the varieties of daffodils in bloom on their estate. Now, these events may seem unrelated, but today they come together each April in a grand celebration, the Daffodil Festival organized by the Tacoma Events Commission, and the Daffodil Marine Regatta sponsored by the Tacoma Yacht Club. Originally the daffodils were raised for the bulbs, and the blossoms were thrown away or used as fertilizer. These days they are not only big business, they decorate the many floats and boats that are part of the festival. The daffodil Royal Court are often seen aboard one of the yachts. The Regatta precedes from the Yacht Club Basin down the waterfront just past the end of Restaurant Row. There the Princess boat is positioned, and participating boats recognize the princesses with a courtly wave, turn to port, and then depart for home. ◼

If it's the last weekend in February, its bluegrass time in Tacoma. Since 1994, the Wintergrass Festival brings out bluegrass and acoustic musicians, like the Randy Kohrs Band, who jam for the crowds with their string instruments. Recognized as the first winter bluegrass festival in the country, Wintergrass is somewhat of a family reunion. Year after year, musicians who are both related by blood and related by a passion for acoustic sound return to play. Bluegrass is renowned as multigenerational music. "One of the things that makes Wintergrass great is that probably 75 percent of the people who come here are players themselves. It's a real players' festival," says Patrice O'Neil of Acoustic Sound, the nonprofit organization that founded and continues to produce the annual event. And in keeping with the bluegrass spirit, plenty of workshops are offered for interested participants, featuring tips on everything from stage fright to clogging, and from beginning mandolin to master fiddle. ■

Franke Tobey Jones's twenty-acre campus is ideally located in the north end of Tacoma with picturesque fountains, walking paths, well-maintained grounds and gardens, beautiful Tudor-estate buildings, and waterviews for all to enjoy. It's retirement with all the amenities desired for senior living.

Franke Tobey Jones Offers an Array of Amenities to Residents

Independence, wellness, community involvement, and an enriching lifestyle. Since 1924, Franke Tobey Jones Continuing Care Retirement Community has offered those important qualities to seniors. From independent retirement living to twenty-four-hour skilled health care, Franke Tobey Jones stands for a tradition of excellence. Founded as a nonprofit retirement community, it is now a public charity providing support and outreach on campus and in the community.

The twenty-acre estate has new condo-style apartments, duplexes, and the historic Tobey Jones building for independent living; the Lillian Pratt building for assisted living; the Health Care Center skilled nursing facility; and "Our Place," a memory care unit.

Franke Tobey Jones provides many other services such as a concierge and receptionist to help with transportation, travel, and personal and business needs. Guest facilities are available for visitors. There is also a large resident

---

From independent retirement living to twenty-four-hour skilled health care, Franke Tobey Jones stands for a tradition of excellence.

---

garden area and greenhouse, or residents can share in the work of the campus gardens. Another recent addition is the woodshop and hobby/craft areas.

One of the most popular and noteworthy services is the MJ Wicks Family Wellness Center with an indoor walking track, exercise equipment, daily classes, personal training, and more. Wellness living provides the opportunity for campus residents and community seniors to live independently as long as possible.

Whether they are physical, intellectual, spiritual, social, or entertainment activities, there is something for everyone to enrich life at Franke Tobey Jones. ■

It is a Tacoma landmark that has been around since 1927 when it opened as the Coffee Pot Restaurant. Over the years it has operated as a food drive-thru and a speakeasy. In 1955, Bob and Lylabell Radonich bought the restaurant, and Lylabell concocted the name from a lyric in a popular Ink Spots song. Bob transformed the interior to cater to new audiences as a music club in the sixties. At one time it had a Polynesian theme with a Jungle Room and two chimpanzees called—what else?—Java and Jive. Through good times and bad, urban renewal and rescue, and even near misses with fire, Bob's "World Famous" Java Jive has stood its ground at the end of South Tacoma Way for over seventy-five years. Today it has finally achieved official historical status through the city, and the twenty-five-foot-high concrete structure still proudly welcomes visitors. ■

| Photo by **David Gibb** |

| Photo by **David Gibb** |

The sign alone is enough to make most people's mouths water. And if that doesn't do it, the pink tin and the fancy gold foil that surround each confection surely will. Almond Roca Buttercrunch starts with a buttercrunch center made with real vanilla and butter created especially for Brown & Haley. Since they do not add salt or water to their buttercrunch, the texture is crunchy with a soft bite. The center is coated with the rich flavor of chocolate made from cocoa beans from around the world, then topped with fresh—not roasted—almonds for a softer, more delicate flavor. The candy has been around since 1923, when Harry Brown developed a recipe for the first log-shaped candy, which has become a worldwide favorite. Almond Roca was the first candy to be put in a sealed tin. Tins of the candy were shipped to troops during World War II, and the secret was out. Today it can be found on retail shelves in thirty-five countries on six continents. Almond Roca is still being made with the same care in the same factory where it all started. ■

| Photo by **David Gibb** |

Mixing form and function, color and transparency, the Chihuly Bridge of Glass is a striking art object that also serves as a pedestrian bridge. Conceived by native glass artist Dale Chihuly and commissioned by Tacoma's Museum of Glass, the five-hundred-foot-long bridge links downtown Tacoma to the city's waterfront. The bridge is divided into three main sections, including the eighty-foot-high Venetian Wall (shown here), which serves as a giant display case for 109 of Chihuly's vivid glass sculptures. During the day the Venetian Wall is a spectacular display of color and form, while at night, fiber optic lights create an entirely different visual experience. ■

A longshore worker prepares for offloading containers at the Port of Tacoma.

| Photo by **Doug Bond** |

Port of Tacoma Is Major Force in Local and Regional Economy

Over the years, the Port of Tacoma, located on Commencement Bay in southern Puget Sound, has developed both as a major international port and a major force in the local and regional economy. It is now one of the leading international ports on the West Coast and one of the top-ten container ports in North America. It is also appropriately called the economic engine of Pierce County.

The establishment of the Port of Tacoma in 1918 by a vote of the citizens of Pierce County followed Washington state's 1911 passage of a law that allowed counties to establish public port districts. Prior to that time, most of Tacoma's shipping facilities were privately owned by the railroads. Starting out on 240 acres in 1919, the port grew quickly and exponentially, not only in terms of its physical holdings, but also in the amount of global maritime trade that occurs there.

On average, the port handles more than $35 billion in international trade each year with a vast array of countries worldwide. Japan, China, and South Korea are among the port's leading trading partners. In addition, more than $3 billion in goods makes its way between Alaska and the Port of Tacoma each year. Served by Horizon Lines and Totem Ocean Trailer Express (TOTE), the port is the gateway to Alaska.

On average, the port handles more than $35 billion in international trade each year with a vast array of countries worldwide.

From automobiles and bulk cargoes to breakbulk, heavy-lift, and project cargoes, the port's diverse facilities allow it to respond to the varied import and export needs of its extensive list of customers, which encompasses many of the top container shipping lines in the world, including Evergreen, Hyundai, "K" Line, Maersk, and Yang Ming.

To further enhance its role as a major shipping center, the Port of Tacoma also boasts first-rate connections to inland transportation networks. With four dockside intermodal rail yards, switching and terminal rail service, and access to major interstate freeways, the port is able to help customers move cargo quickly and seamlessly toward its destination. Each year, the port invests millions of dollars into expanding its facilities and transportation connections to meet the growth needs of its existing customers and potential customers.

| Photo by **Jackson Hill** |

The substantial activity at the port also has a major effect on the local economy and the community-at-large. More than 43,000 jobs in Pierce County, as well as over 113,000 jobs in Washington state, are related to the Port of Tacoma's activities. The port's economic activity also generates taxes at the local, county, and state government levels, which ultimately benefits schools and civic organizations, among other entities. In addition to dedicating itself to boosting industrial development and attracting major manufacturing centers to the region, the port also focuses on environmental stewardship, investing millions of dollars to protect and improve Commencement Bay and its surrounding waters.

The Port of Tacoma continues to build for the future to meet the needs of its customers, creating jobs for citizens and expanding business and trade opportunities for companies throughout the region. ■

The Yang Ming's night lights
reflect off the water at Port of
Tacoma's newest terminal: the
Olympic Container Terminal,
operated by the Yang Ming Line.

The exterior of Sanford & Son Antiques and Auctions does not adequately prepare visitors for what is to be found inside. This huge warehouse has floor after floor and room after room filled to capacity with antiques of every possible description. One of the most unusual articles to be auctioned recently was a Foton 6 satellite. This Soviet spacecraft circled the Earth with French experiments on a fifteen-day unmanned mission, traveled 7.4 million miles, landed in Siberia, and ultimately found its way to Sanford & Son and auctioneer Alan Gorsuch. Curiosity seekers wishing to visit this unusual establishment along Tacoma's Antique Row on Broadway between Ninth and Seventh streets need not travel so far. A quick ride on Tacoma's Link light rail will get them there in no time. By the way, be sure to ask for a look at the owner's mint-condition black and yellow 1955 Buick convertible. ∎

One of Tacoma's architectural treasures, the colorful, wedge-shaped Bostwick Building received new life after renovations were completed in 2000. The former 1889 hotel now houses twenty studio and one-bedroom apartments on its upper floors, while its lower level is home to various retail establishments, including a Tully's Coffee. A regional franchise based in Seattle, Tully's Coffee offers gourmet coffee, tea and juice drinks, plus a variety of pastries and other baked goods. Wi-Fi, live music, and open mic Fridays make it a favorite neighborhood hangout. ■

| Photo by **Eric Francis** |

Tacoma Electric Supply operates ten trucks daily throughout the Puget Sound region. With a fleet of twenty-four-foot flatbeds and the company's signature "Red Dot" delivery service trucks, they are sure to have what's right for the job.

Tacoma Electric Supply Strives to Outpace Competitors

When it first opened its doors on May 1, 1981, Tacoma Electric Supply employed three people, including its founder, Randy Mauermann. Today, the company has grown to include two locations and over seventy employees. It is also consistently listed among the top 200 largest distributors in the nation by *Electrical Wholesaling* magazine.

But Tacoma Electric Supply's mission is not to be the biggest, but the best. With its low employee turnover, high customer retention, and a sustained annual growth rate of 20 percent in the new millennium, Tacoma Electric Supply consistently outpaces the competition.

Key to the company's success is its dedication to three core business values: cultivating loyal employees through rewarding career opportunities, attracting loyal customers through the best products and service available, and contributing to the future growth and stability of the surrounding communities.

Under the direction of Randy Mauermann and his sons, Kevin and Brian, Tacoma Electric Supply ensures the future health of the company by training its employees today. "Many companies don't plan for their youth moving up through the ranks," says Kevin. "But we invest very heavily in what we consider our most important asset by giving our employees the tools they need to be successful in a very fast-paced, ever-changing environment."

> *"Whatever our customers need, we make sure it's always on our shelves," says Kevin. "After all, we're in the business of distribution."*

Training ranges from internships with local universities to in-house seminars to job shadowing with senior members. It's the kind of care and attention that ensures Tacoma Electric one of the highest employee retention rates in the industry.

The same approach results in exceptional customer service. With a seventy-thousand-square-foot facility in Tacoma and a new location in Puyallup that includes a fourteen-hundred-square-foot showroom, Tacoma Electric Supply features an extensive product line of everything from wire to hardware to service equipment.

"Whatever our customers need, we make sure it's always on our shelves," says Kevin. "After all, we're in the business of distribution."

Part of that business includes backing up the company's products with a scanning system that represents the state-of-the-art in warehouse inventory control technology. Further, a trained sales force is available to assist clients with every phase of their project, from bid preparation to delivery.

Tacoma Electric Supply is also dedicated to a variety of community development efforts. Employees play an active role in the Tacoma/Pierce County Chamber of Commerce, the Rotary Club, and the Coalition for Nalley Valley Business Development. Philanthropic efforts include cochairing with city council members various committees to help address the needs of Tacoma's homeless. The company also contributes assets to the Point Defiance Zoo and Aquarium's annual fundraiser, Zoobilee; local elementary school food programs; and the Tacoma Rescue Mission.

As a fixture in downtown Tacoma for over twenty-five years, Tacoma Electric Supply is proud to be a part of the city's transformation and to help establish a prosperous community both inside and outside the company's walls. ■

Purchasing agent Stan Forbus (left) and senior sales associate Bill Cunningham (right) assist an electrical contractor in determining the correct heat loss calculation. This kind of personal service has been a trademark of the company since it first opened.

| Photo by **Eric Francis** |

They move quietly and efficiently, these modern versions of streetcars. While new Tacoma's Link light rail line is the first electric light rail line in the state, its roots go back to the days of the streetcar pulled through Old Town. The line is tailor-made for transportation in downtown, connecting passengers from the many museums, shops, and restaurants through an intermodal station at the Tacoma Dome, where commuters can catch buses and other trains for destinations beyond. ■

Thanks to Tacoma's accessible light rail system, you can leave your car at home when traveling to and from downtown. Or forgo the mechanical transport altogether in favor of old-fashioned foot power. Not only is downtown the center of commerce and culture, the area is also highly bikeable and walkable, with wide sidewalks, recreational trails, and walking paths like the Chihuly Bridge of Glass linking major areas and attractions. ■

| Photo by **Sonja Hall** |

| Photo by **Jackson Hill** |

For members throughout Tacoma, TAPCO Credit Union' main branch on Nineteenth Street is the place to go for all of their financial needs. From accounts to loans, the staff that works here is dedicated to helping members effectively manage their fiscal activities.

TAPCO Offers Top-Notch Member Care and Financial Services

In 1934, nine City of Tacoma employees decided to take control of their financial affairs while helping their coworkers, friends, and loved ones do the same. The result of their endeavor was TAPCO Credit Union, a not-for-profit cooperative institution that today serves twenty-five thousand members throughout Tacoma–Pierce County with a full suite of financial services, and the oldest financial institution in Pierce County.

From checking, savings, and money market accounts to car, home, and business loans, TAPCO provides its members with the tools they need to safely and securely manage their money, complete with competitive rates and low fees. Over time, the organization, with five branches and seventy employees, has enhanced its offerings, regularly adding up-to-date benefits like Internet banking and E-Statements. Yet, one thing has always remained constant at TAPCO: superior, personalized member service. In fact, TAPCO was rated number-one for the best customer service provided by a credit union in Pierce County.

"Our members are our top priority, and we strive to take excellent care of them," says John Bechtholt, CEO. "That's why TAPCO Credit Union maintains a friendly environment in which each member can feel comfortable with us handling their confidential transactions, knowing that our door is always open."

> *"Our members are our top priority, and we strive to take excellent care of them," says John Bechtholt, CEO.*

This supportive approach extends to the community, where TAPCO sponsors local events and spearheads fund-raising initiatives for the Mary Bridge Children's Hospital, the American Cancer Society, and the American Heart Association, among others. The reason is simple. According to Bechtholt, "TAPCO's membership is our community, and it's our philosophy to always give back." ■

| Photo by **Eric Francis** |

Whether paddling in Commencement Bay with the city of Tacoma in the background, or exploring the marine life in the shallow and clear waters in other areas of Puget Sound, sea kayakers say that one of the reasons they love their sport is that it allows them to paddle in places where others can't. Rhonda Schwab (red kayak), a member of the Mountaineers Sea Kayaking Group and the Washington Kayak Club, spends nearly every weekend on the water. "There is something special about being on the water and looking out to see the mountains, or watching the wind dance on top of the water creating waves," she says. A certified British Canoe Union (BCU) Level Two coach and American Canoe Association (ACA) certified instructor on open water and surf, Schwab also enjoys parlaying her knowledge and passion for paddling to teaching newcomers. "I love teaching people kayaking skills so that they will be safe and have fun. The views we have here in Washington are magnificent. You just have to get out in your kayak and try it." ■

Commercial account representatives, specializing in the transportation industry, discuss the best options for delivering certificates of coverage quickly and accurately. Weekly staff meetings also allow employees to touch base with colleagues and stay up-to-date on coverage and service topics.

Brown & Brown Offers Effective Solutions for Every Challenge

As the nation's sixth-largest independent insurance broker, Brown & Brown, Inc. has offices throughout the United States, including Tacoma and Seattle. A standout for combining local traditions of responsiveness, technical competence, and quality service with the advantages of a national parent company, Brown & Brown Tacoma provides for the most demanding insurance needs.

But the firm's success is not based solely on selling insurance. Instead, the primary goal is to craft relationships. Brown & Brown calls it The Power of We—a team of seasoned professionals working closely with clients to assess their needs and create effective solutions for both present and future challenges.

Central to the firm's high standard of service is a series of guiding principles governing employee/employee and employee/client relationships. Called "Our Promises," they reflect a commitment to responsive and responsible service and respectful, caring interactions.

With experts in every discipline of the insurance brokerage industry, Brown & Brown excels in employee benefits programs, property and casualty insurance, and personal auto and home insurance. The firm's high level of technical competence ensures clients the best rates available, as well as the coverage that most closely matches their needs. Likewise, Brown & Brown provides a host of support services for its clients, including educational seminars, compliance alert notifications, and personalized client Web sites.

Called "Our Promises," they reflect a commitment to responsive and responsible service and respectful, caring interactions.

With a history in Tacoma–Pierce County going back over one hundred years, Brown & Brown is committed to sharing its personal and corporate resources. Associates sit on no fewer than twenty local community service organizations, while others direct the firm's standing committee, MEET A Promise, which provides many hands-on community service opportunities each year and makes monthly and quarterly donations to various nonprofits. Brown & Brown is also a major contributor to the United Way of Pierce County, and the yearly contributions made by the firm and by employee donation drives have earned it United Way Top 25 Partner Awards.

Brown & Brown is consistently recognized in its roles as both a top insurance intermediary and a community partner. Earning a reputation as the "Broker of Due Diligence" in service standards and business practices by annual exposure reviews, carrier financial ratings, compensation disclosures, and client report cards, the firm enjoys a better than 90 percent customer retention rate. *Forbes* also ranks Brown & Brown nationally among "America's Best Small Companies," and *Fortune* rates the firm among "America's 100 Fastest-Growing Companies."

Locally, Brown & Brown Tacoma was chosen as one of four outstanding retail offices recognized by Brown & Brown, Inc. in its 2005 Annual Report. It has also received the Community Service Award by the Association of Washington Business over the past three years. And in 2006 the United Way once again recognized its prodigious efforts with its Small Business Partner of the Year award.

More than just a broker, Brown & Brown strives to build lasting partnerships and forge a legacy of excellence that benefits the entire Tacoma–Pierce County community, and Puget Sound and Pacific Northwest area. ■

These account executives specialize in employee benefits, including medical, dental, prescription, vision, group life, and income protection. Here they are working on ideas to refresh and enhance client Web site tools.

| Photo by **Eric Francis** |

| Photo by **Eric Francis** |

No need to book a tropical vacation to experience the wonders of marine life. Everything from whales and sharks to sea urchins and starfish can be viewed up close and personal at Point Defiance Zoo and Aquarium. Established in 1905 and located on twenty-nine acres overlooking Puget Sound, Point Defiance serves as a vital discovery, conservation, and learning center for the animals and plant life native to Pacific Rim countries. Currently, it is the only facility in the region to house beluga whales, Pacific walrus, and a variety of large shark species. Committed to conservation efforts both at home and abroad, the zoo has become a national leader in captive breeding and reintroduction efforts for endangered red wolves, helping to grow the population from 14 wolves in 1980 to over 250 today. The zoo also sponsors a variety of kids' programs, including summer camps and the new Kids' Zone, a hands-on activity center that teaches young children about animals and their care. ■

| Photo by **Eric Francis** |

| Photo by **Eric Francis** |

The largest paper machine at Simpson Tacoma Kraft Company, LLC, uses complex computer calculations to vary the "recipes" for two hundred customer orders. Paper stock starts as 99.5 percent water and results in two-ply, heavy liner-board paper used to make boxes.

| Photo by **Jackson Hill** |

Simpson Helps to Improve Quality of Life

At Simpson we use every part of the tree except its shadow. "That's what the modern, high-tech wood products industry is all about," said Ray Tennison, president of Simpson Investment Company. "Our lumber mills use laser-guided saws to make sure we get the most value from every log. Residual wood chips are used in our pulp and paper mill to make linerboard for boxes. Bark is sold for use in landscaping, and sawdust is sold to make particleboard. Recently, we started recycling the wood waste ash from the pulping process. We recycle it to companies who add it to other aggregate ingredients in concrete."

Founded in 1890, Simpson is one of the oldest continuously operating forest products companies in the Pacific Northwest. With headquarters in Tacoma, there are three operating subsidiaries: Simpson Timber Company, Simpson Door Company, and Simpson Tacoma Kraft Company, LLC.

"Because we're a privately held company, we don't focus on quarterly reports. Our owners take the long-term view in our operations and in supporting organizations in the communities we call home," Tennison said.

Simpson's commitment to higher education, especially in the areas of math and science, is a good example. The company regularly supports internship programs in the community. At the higher education level, Tennison has chaired capital campaigns for the University of Washington–Tacoma, and Simpson has supported community colleges as well.

> *"Our owners take the long-term view in our operations and in supporting organizations in the communities we call home," Tennison said.*

Going "beyond compliance" to be good stewards of the environment is another integral part of planning at Simpson. "At our paper mill in Tacoma, we have invested $300 million to clean up the shoreline and reduce odorous emissions, as well as improve manufacturing processes," Tennison explained. "Over the past sixteen years, our conservation programs have reduced freshwater usage by 65 percent. The EPA recognized our company for going beyond the legal requirements and making a public commitment to reducing pollution." Simpson is also in the forefront of paper recycling technology. Simpson Tacoma Kraft Company recycles more than five hundred tons of corrugated containers every day.

Still another example of Simpson's good-neighbor policy is the Community Care Team. This group of employees conducts community service projects throughout the year with the solid support of management. Ongoing projects for Community Care volunteers include Helping Hand House, Network Tacoma, and Shared Housing Services.

For more than one hundred years, Simpson has lived up to its mission to improve the quality of life in areas it serves and to be a catalyst for employees to become involved and provide leadership in their communities. ■

Operator Terry Bowington monitors logs through the cut-off saw at Simpson Timber Company's Commencement Bay Operations in Tacoma. The sawmill, completed in 2001, is one of the largest-dimensional lumber mills in North America.

| Photo by **Jackson Hill** |

Houses of Worship

Tacoma's houses of worship are as diverse as their congregants. In structure and style, they range from modern to historic, dramatic to quaint. Built in 1925 in the Romanesque style, the First Presbyterian Church of Tacoma is distinguished by its majestic church tower and dome, which stands 165 feet high. A landmark in earlier years for ships entering Tacoma's harbor, the dome is decorated with mosaics of Christian symbols from churches around the world, while the windows above the choir loft are masterpieces of stained-glass artistry. No less masterful is the Gothic-style Holy Rosary Catholic Church, which also operates the city's oldest parochial school, first established in 1891. Erected in 1872, Old St. Peter's Episcopal Church reminds us in another way of the persistence of faith: as a self-supporting community church, it receives no denominational support; its clergy is all-volunteer; and the building itself, while a historical landmark, is maintained entirely through the support of its congregation. ■

| Photo by **Jackson Hill** |

The Double Four Tree Farm, established in 1981, is a family business owned by Bob and Jan Moore that caters to folks in the Tacoma area who like to cut their own Christmas trees. The twenty-two-acre tree farm in South Pierce County has more than twenty thousand cultured trees to choose from. And just to make sure there is an ongoing supply for future generations, approximately thirty-five hundred seedlings are planted each year. "We've been here long enough to see children grow up and come back to choose a tree with their own children," said Jan. Those going home with a tree get some tips to make them last. "For one thing, we tell them before putting up the tree, make a fresh cut so it can absorb water," said Bob. (An average tree may consume between a quart and a gallon of water per day.) With proper care, a fresh tree will easily last thirty days. Since picking exactly the right tree takes time, there is always free hot coffee and apple cider brewing. Smart shoppers know to avoid the rush by preselecting their tree in November, decorating it with colored ribbon—which is provided—and coming back to cut it later. ■

| Photo by **Jackson Hill** |

Curious about how these magnificent animals live in the wild? Northwest Trek and Wildlife Park allows you to witness their daily habits. Established in 1975, thanks to a generous donation of land by Dr. David Hellyer and his wife, Connie, the 715-acre Northwest Trek Wildlife Park serves as a vital sanctuary to over two hundred native animals representing thirty different species. Take the park's signature tram tour over 435 acres of wetlands, forests, and meadows, and experience an hour's worth of up-close, free-roaming wildlife viewing that includes moose and mountain goat, bald eagles and barn owls, brown and black bear, and even native wild cats like bobcat, cougar, and lynx. A walking tour along well-defined trails affords even closer glimpses of otter, badger, wolves, and if you're lucky, a wolverine kit. Born on Valentine's Day 2006 the baby female is the first wolverine born to Northwest Trek and only the second born in captivity to a North American–accredited zoo since 2004. ∎

| Photo by **Alan S. Weiner**

| Photo by **Alan S. Weiner** |

| Photo by **David Gibb** |

| Photo by **David Gibb** |

From May through October, visitors and residents alike flock to the Proctor Farmers Market held every Saturday. From fresh produce and flowers to hand-crafted items and free live music, there is something for everyone. The market has been open over a decade, and each year new vendors join regulars who come back season after season. Sponsored by the Proctor District Association, the market has a three-point mission: to connect local farmers and their farm-fresh produce with Tacoma's North End community, to enhance the local community by providing a pleasant environment for people to show, and to support the local retail community. A highlight each year is berry season when Puyallup Valley strawberries, raspberries, and blackberries are plentiful. Eastern Washington growers also bring in their Bing and Rainier cherries, which are always a crowd pleaser. And of course there is an abundance of cauliflower, broccoli, spinach, peas, peppers, and tomatoes, and annuals, perennials, and exotics of all kinds. ■

| Photo by **Michael Marl** |

Cushioning Your Assets since 1946

Innovation is alive and well at Tacoma's family-owned Comfor Products, Inc. Founded in 1946 Comfor Products is celebrating sixty years in the specialty foam business this year. The company has evolved dramatically over the last six decades, but with all of its changes foam has always been at the core of its business.

"Ralph Smalling along with his wife Dorothy founded the company originally known as Industrial Rubber & Supply, Inc.," explains Scott Smalling, CEO. "My grandfather started the company selling rubber boots and hoses as a distributor for BF Goodrich. When BF Goodrich started pouring latex foam rubber, Ralph quickly seized the opportunity to become the first company to distribute and fabricate latex foam in the Northwest," Smalling added. Latex foam rubber, still in use today, is a renewable resource and the world's finest natural foam cushioning.

As the foam market matured, the company evolved to service the growing furniture industry in the Northwest. When Jay Smalling, Scott's father, graduated from college and returned from a tour in the U.S. Navy he added his own ideas to continue to grow the family business.

> *"We're the most technologically advanced, consumer-friendly bedding manufacturer in the world," says Smalling.*

The company's largest concentration of customers in the 1960s were furniture and auto upholsterers, and Jay's vision was to become a one-stop source for these customers. Throughout the '60s and '70s Jay developed a line of upholstery fabrics, vinyls, and supplies. Jay continued to expand this division well into the 1990s, sourcing new products, buying merchandise, and designing most of the sample books used to sell fabrics to the consumers through their retail upholstery partners.

In the mid-'90s, when Scott was cutting his teeth in the business, he saw a need to create divisions that were more representative of the markets in which they were focused. Along with Scott's wife, Carolyn, they created Carl Havens Signature Fabrics to further penetrate the wholesale fabric market, including hotels, restaurants, and assisted-living centers. Carolyn quickly took over this division and started designing her own exclusive fabric lines, incorporating a proprietary new process called Crypton®. Carolyn was instrumental in helping the Crypton® brand push the envelope on innovation while that company was in its infancy. Crypton® is now marketed around the globe with sales in excess of $50 million annually.

In 2003 the company began another metamorphosis. "We've taken our years of expertise in the foam and the fabric business and dovetailed the two divisions to produce a revolutionary fabric-sided foam bed," said Smalling. "It just made sense." The bedding industry, long dominated in North American by one technology, inner springs, is undergoing a dramatic change.

The new specialty category (in which Comfor-Pedic™ is a major player) is currently just 5 percent of the overall bedding market, but growing at a staggering 51 percent per year.

Smalling and Jack Squires, president, are the leaders of Comfor Products. Comfor material is the company's unique, proprietary formulation created by Smalling and Squires. This creation, along with many other patented advantages, sets Comfor-Pedic™ apart in the market.

"Our Comfor Material is as unique as our dedication to consumer comfort and safety," explained Squires. "We pride ourselves on never settling; we constantly push the envelope in all areas of the business."

| Continued on page 104 |

Ralph Smalling, Founder

Jay Smalling, Retired

Scott Smalling, CEO

| Photo by **Jackson Hill** |

| Continued from page 103 |

| Photo by **Michael Marl** |

"In summary, we're the most technologically advanced, consumer-friendly bedding manufacturer in the world," says Smalling. "We have sixty years of experience in the comfort business, and we have put all the experience to use in creating Comfor-Pedic™." The fact that the company has a less than 1 percent return rate on its bedding products certainly backs up his claim. While Comfor-Pedic™ could be called a Cinderella story, the founding philosophies and the grit on which the company was founded in the 1940s still ring true—constantly striving to provide consumers with the very best and setting the standard for the industry. ■

| Photo by **David Gibb** |

| Photo by **David Gibb** |

Y ou gotta love a festival where you can stuff yourself silly on Funnel Cake and soft serve one minute and sample regional wines and savory fare the next. Held each year at Point Defiance Park over three days the last weekend of June, the Taste of Tacoma acquaints attendees with the best food and drink in the area. In 2006, twenty-eight restaurants and twenty food vendors plied their fare, everything from ethnic to all-American, while musical groups of all varieties entertained the crowd from three stages. And unlike many outdoor festivals, traffic isn't much of a problem. Not only does a round-trip fare from TCC Transit Center to Point Defiance currently stand at one dollar, you can also bike or skate there from almost any point in the city and leave your wheels at the festival's secured bicycle corral. ▪

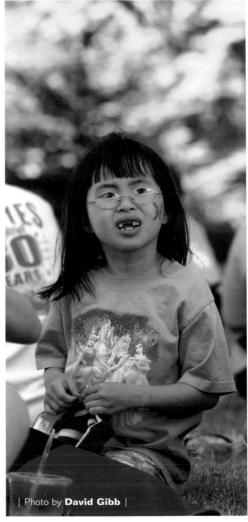

| Photo by **David Gibb** |

| Photo by **Jim Bryant** |

| Photo by **David Gibb** |

Quilts have always been associated with warmth and comfort, but these "Comfort Quilts" provide a special kind of coziness. Each year quilters like Conni Smith volunteer through the Gig Harbor Quilt Festival to collect a carful of donated quilts to take to oncologists' offices to give to patients going through chemotherapy. "We haven't quite filled the car yet," said Ione Whitney, another volunteer, "but at the last event we collected sixty quilts, and that's quite a lot." Created in 2000, the four-day Gig Harbor Quilt Festival coincides with Cancer Awareness month. Participants can enjoy quilting classes and workshops with nationally known teachers as well as explore the maritime history, scenery, shops, and restaurants—many of whom are supporters—in Gig Harbor. "In addition to the Comfort Quilts, we invite local artists to make and donate quilts which we auction to raise money to support breast cancer research." To date, the festival has raised one hundred thousand dollars. ■

Gig Harbor

| Photo by **Eric Francis** |

Tucked-away towns can be a tourist's treasure, and Gig Harbor is certainly one of those towns. First named in 1941 by the commander of the U.S. Exploring Expedition, Captain Charles Wilkes, the inlet cover in Puget Sound served as safe shelter from a storm by several of the expedition's longboats and the captain's smaller boat—the "gig." Abundant with nature's riches of land and sea, Gig Harbor drew many settlers from Norway, Sweden, and Croatia, who made a living in fishing, boat building, and operating sawmills. Today, picture-perfect Gig Harbor, with Mount Rainier majestically rising in the background, attracts visitors who enjoy the town's nautical charm and history, as well as the specialty shops, art galleries, restaurants, and bed-and-breakfasts. As the southern gateway to the Kitsap and Olympic peninsulas, Gig Harbor is just across the mile-long suspended Tacoma Narrows Bridge, less than ten miles from that city. ■

| Photo by **Eric Francis** |

"King" Oscar Hokold,
still young at ninety-one.

| Photo by **Alan S. Weiner** |

Oscar Hokold: A Man of Integrity and Vision for the Future

Oscar Hokold is "king" of many castles, although the humble builder who claims he is "just an average person is who well blessed" would refute that moniker. Nearly everywhere you look in Tacoma, there's a building that exists because of the Tacoma native's vision and hard work. "The growth of the south end of Tacoma is a direct result of Oscar," says Linda Acosta, general manager of Hokold Development. "He's a self-made man who never gives up."

A true renaissance man, Hokold has been a commercial fisherman, a logger, a marine pipe fitter, and a contractor—all trades that require hands-on skills. "I've worked hard, and I've tried to do it in an honest, Christian manner," he says. "My first job of any consequence involved logging in Washington. The wages were poor, but the humility and the kindness of working with others helped to build character." More than seventy-five years later, his integrity remains. "I'm just happy he's stayed here this long, because he's such a good citizen," says Jack Fabulich, former commissioner of the Port of Tacoma. "I've known him for more than forty years. He's done a lot of great things for this area, particularly for the military. He's an excellent builder who loves community involvement."

> *"The growth of the south end of Tacoma is a direct result of Oscar,"*
> *says Linda Acosta, general manager of Hokold Development.*

Hokold's first foray in housing construction came around the time of World War II. Fresh from commercial fishing in Alaska, and newly married to his lifelong partner Olivann, Hokold took a job with a prominent Tacoma builder to construct a single home. He continued in the home building industry for a while until he decided that a position as a pipe fitter for Todd Pacific Shipyards might be a more stable income for the newlyweds. However, his self-starting trait resurfaced, and he decided to return to construction. He purchased a lot, built a house, and immediately sold it for a small profit. He bought two more lots and began building in the north end of the city. At the time, the south end of Tacoma was farmland, but Hokold saw it from a different perspective. "I bought property that no one else wanted. Every banker in Tacoma thought I was crazy, but I stayed with it. It's been quite successful," he says.

"Successful" is an understatement. From homes to apartments, and then from condominiums to motels/convention centers, the construction icon, who is still going strong in his nineties, has built an empire: Hokold Development. In addition to the more than two thousand apartment units he's built, some of the most recognizable properties are the King Oscar Tacoma Inn, Motels and Convention Centers. Conveniently located off Interstate 5 and within minutes of McChord Air Force Base, Fort Lewis, and Pacific Lutheran University,

| Continued on page 110 |

The warmth of the King Oscar Tacoma Inn is evident the moment customers check in at the front desk.

| Photo by **Alan S. Weiner** |

Between the neighboring motel and the Inn, the King Oscar Tacoma has 375 guest rooms and over ten thousand square feet of meeting space.

| Photo by **Alan S. Weiner** |

| Continued from page 109 |

the facilities draw both business and leisure travelers. All five locations feature signature "royal treatment" customer service amenities: executive suites, a deluxe complimentary continental breakfast, meeting facilities, complimentary airport shuttle service, ample free parking, and competitive rates. The convention centers offer more than ten thousand square feet of flexible and professional meeting space.

While it would seem natural that Hokold would do what most people work a lifetime to do—that is, retire comfortably—he prefers otherwise. "Mr. Hokold's work is so important to him. He comes in every day," says Acosta, who has worked with him since 1987. "I believe the main reason he's continued to build his company is to keep all of his employees employed. He wants to be sure that they can continue to take care of their own families." ■

A group of friends gathers to enjoy their dining experience at Oscar's Restaurant & Lounge on Hosmer, located between the King Oscar Tacoma Inn and King Oscar Motel.

| Photo by **Alan S. Weiner** |

Every neighborhood needs a local hangout, and in Tacoma's university area, that hangout is the Swiss Pub. Established in 1913, the venue has become popular not only with the college crowd, but with adults of all ages who appreciate great pub fare, a wide selection of beer and specialty drinks, and rockin' music most nights of the week. The pub is also an art gallery, featuring revolving exhibitions by local artists as well as a permanent collection over its antique bar of patron Dave Chihuly's glass sculptures. ■

Before the days of Prohibition, Tacoma was a serious brewing town with roots that go back to some of the original inhabitants who studied the time-honored methods of German brew masters. Pacific Brewing & Malting Company did not survive the anti-alcohol movement, but when it closed down, it was the largest brewery in Tacoma and the second-largest in the state behind Seattle Brewing & Malting, maker of Rainier. Founded by German immigrant Anton Huth, the company brewed one beer labeled two ways, Pacific Beer for locals and Tacoma Beer for markets across the western United States and the Pacific Rim, with the slogan, "Best, East or West." Pacific Beer was bottled in quarts and pints, served in bars and restaurants, and delivered to homes by the case. Today residents and visitors alike can find a wide selection of brews made by the various brewpubs around town. The first one, Engine House No. 9, opened in 1995. Judging from E-9's Tacoma Brew, the past has just caught up with the present. ■

The popular Puyallup Fair Concert Series has been sponsored by Columbia Bank since 1997. The series brings scores of diverse musical acts to the people of the Northwest. Like the fair itself, community involvement is a tradition for Columbia Bank.

Columbia Bank—Where Community and Personal Service Count

At Columbia Bank, people bank with people, not with bricks and mortar or machines. While Columbia has all of the technology to provide the broad range of products and services of a much larger bank, it also has something few big banks have—a business philosophy that truly focuses on exceptional service, for both customers and the community.

"We began with the philosophy to provide a local, customer-focused approach to doing business, coupled with all the modern conveniences—including people," says Melanie Dressel, president and CEO. "Columbia bankers work closely with their customers, emphasizing personalized, local decision making. That philosophy continues to guide us today."

> *"We began with the philosophy to provide a local, customer-focused approach to doing business, coupled with all the modern conveniences."*

Columbia bankers are not only in the business of providing outstanding service and personalized products, but are also strongly committed to the communities they serve. Charitable contributions and sponsorships are focused on youth programs, community revitalization, individual and community health, and the arts. Bank volunteers are involved in countless programs throughout the year that are as diverse as the people they serve.

"We have certainly grown, both in size and in profitability," notes Dressel. "What hasn't changed is who we are. We have stayed true to our conviction that our real strength lies in providing exceptional service to our customers

| Continued on page 114 |

Columbia Bank's headquarters, the Columbia Bank Center, is a unique and familiar downtown Tacoma landmark. Evocative of Tacoma's rich maritime history and thriving art culture, the "good ship Columbia" is a symbol of Columbia's commitment to each community it serves.

| Photo by **Alan S. Weiner** |

| Continued from page 113 |

Columbia Bank is a longtime supporter of the Children's Museum of Tacoma and its unique learning environments for children of all ages. Here children learn about buying groceries, running a store and—a Columbia Bank favorite—providing great customer service.

| Photo by **Alan S. Weiner** |

and investing in our people and the communities we serve. We've combined our market savvy and financial expertise with our belief in vital neighborhoods to create programs and services designed to help move our communities forward every day. Our goal is to be the community bank in all the communities we serve."

Columbia Bank is a state-chartered, full-service bank headquartered in Tacoma with assets of almost $2.5 billion and growing. In 1993, Columbia moved its headquarters to downtown Tacoma and began its rapid expansion. From its original four branch offices, Columbia Bank now has almost three dozen in western Washington and plans to expand its geographic footprint. ■

The United Way and Columbia Bank enjoy a long partnership in supporting the communities they serve. "We are only as strong as the communities we serve" is a core principle of both Columbia Bank and the United Way.

| Photo by **Alan S. Weiner** |

| Photo by **David Gibb** |

| Photo by **David Gibb** |

Great steaks, pasta dishes, pizzas, and sandwiches are a few of the reasons the Engine House No. 9 Restaurant and Brewery is consistently rated as one of the top-ten restaurants in Puget Sound. The unique décor is another. Built in 1907 to provide fire protection for Tacoma's North End, E-9 (as it's known locally) still retains many of the building's original elements. Placed on the National Historic Register in 1975, E-9 was renovated into a micro-brewery in 1992 and was the first nonsmoking pub in Pierce County. With two levels and a lovely outdoor patio, E-9 is a scenic and relaxing spot to enjoy one of the award-winning brewery's ten handcrafted ales, as well as imported beers, fine wines, and a large selection of spirits. ■

Four generations of the
Haynes family outside their new
Tacoma office. Left to right:
Brian Haynes, Ben Haynes,
Skip Haynes, and Arne Haynes.

| Photo by **Alan S. Weiner** |

Rainier Connect Makes the Right Calls for Future Success

Sitting in the lobby of Rainier Connect's Tacoma office is a treasured heirloom. It's an authentic Kellogg Switchboard—the actual ring-down telephone machine used by the Christensen family when it assumed Mount Tacoma Telephone and Telegraph in 1912. In those days, the small company, helmed by patriarch "Grandpa Pete" Christensen, provided service to rural customers in Eatonville, Washington, with daughter Annie Christensen Haynes managing up to ten calls at a time on the trusty Kellogg. Times have changed, though, and through five generations of family ownership, what is now Rainier Connect has evolved from a fledgling telephone company into a thriving operation that offers local phone, long distance, cable television, and high-speed Internet services to residential and commercial customers across Tacoma–Pierce County and Lewis County.

"We are dedicated to our customers and their needs," says Arne "Skip" Haynes, who succeeded his father, Arne Haynes, as CEO of Rainier Connect in 1990. "We are a key part of their everyday lives, and we want to serve them in the best way possible."

Fulfilling this mission has called for Rainier Connect, which won the Washington Family Business of the Year award in 2005, to embrace innovation and expand its services regularly over the years. For instance, in 1954, the company converted to dial tone and ultimately became one of the first telephone companies in the state to

> *"…we want to be our customers' preferred provider in an environment that has historically been a monopoly."*

implement digital switching. This forward-thinking approach was never more necessary, however, than with the passing of the Telecommunications Act of 1996, which allowed communications companies to compete in any market. It was then that Skip Haynes decided to prepare Rainier Connect for the twenty-first century through strategic diversification.

"We've had to make the transition from a monopoly organization to a competitive organization," he explains. "We want to be our customers' preferred provider in an environment that has historically been a monopoly."

Therefore, Haynes and Rainier Connect's fifty-eight employees set out to make the company more "datacentric," bringing in new state-of-the-art technologies, adding fiber optic lines throughout the county, and constructing new facilities to ensure that the company would not have to rely on other organizations to provide service. The metamorphosis resulted in Rainier Connect being able to offer enhanced traditional and nontraditional telecommunications services. In fact, Rainier Connect was one of the first telecommunications companies nationwide to furnish 100 percent of its customers with broadband access.

The success experienced by the company made Skip Haynes the perfect candidate to serve as chairman of the board of the United States Telecom Association in 2001. His industry leadership has been an inspiration to his colleagues—just as his company's community involvement serves as an example for the people of Tacoma–Pierce County. From its participation in chamber organizations to its support of local education, Rainier Connect has become one of the area's most dedicated corporate citizens.

"We simply want to be the best we can be," Haynes asserts. "We have a proud history, and we look forward to a rich future." ■

Rainier Connect main office in Eatonville. Technicians are taking customer care representatives on a training day to learn how to install high-speed Internet.

| Photo by **Alan S. Weiner** |

| Photo by **Jim Bryant** |

| Photo by **Jim Bryant** |

With musical roots tracing back to the mid-1940s, the Tacoma Symphony Orchestra entertains the community with concerts ranging from the classics to pops. Each season is unique, each performance moving. The orchestra plays under the careful eye of music director Harvey Felder. As maestro, his energy and baton direct eighty professional musicians in a rich, year-round concert schedule. Known for his commitment to education, the Tacoma Symphony Orchestra's "Simply Symphonic" outreach program for children has flourished under his influence. Assisting Felder is concertmaster Svend Ronning, the first violin chair. Multifaceted in its duties, the responsibilities of the concertmaster include tuning the orchestra in the beginning of the performance and ensuring the nuances of pitch and the overall unity for ideal sound throughout the concert. The concertmaster is the first person to the left of the conductor from the audience's vantage point and is generally the last musician to be seated on stage. ■

Tacoma's urban renewal is closely linked to the rejuvenation of its arts and cultural scene, with top priority given to reestablishing the city's theatrical district as the heart of downtown. It began in 1975 with the restoration of the historic Pantages Theater, which reopened in 1983. That restoration in turn inspired the refurbishment in 1991 of the beautiful 1918 Beaux-Arts Rialto Theater. Then the city purchased the air rights above the Pierce Transit bus turnaround facility, which allowed for the construction of the Theater on the Square performance center and its public park, a popular outdoor gathering spot and venue. During summer nights Theater on the Square Park shows outdoor movies, projected onto the wall of the nearby Woolworth's building. Another distinctive feature of the park is its sculpture, *Canned Salmon*, which was created by Tacoma artists Chris Wooten and Vladimir Shakov and is made of thousands of recycled aluminum cans. ■

Photo by **Sonja Hall** |

The romance. The deception. The tragedy. All this and more was brought vividly to life in Tacoma Opera Association's 2006 production of *La Boheme*. Since 1968 the organization has made going to the opera an exciting and entertaining experience, attracting audiences from throughout Washington, Oregon, and British Columbia. Offering two to three dynamic productions per season at the city's landmark Pantages Theater, the company regularly hosts top-rate artists from throughout the United States. Seeking to heighten awareness and accessibility of the musical arts, the company's original mandate was to perform in English. In 2002, the company began to perform in the operas' original languages, while also offering English supertitles. ■

| Photo by **Jim Bryant** |

The state-of-the-art, roll-on/roll-off vessel *MV Midnight Sun* arrives for her weekly call in Tacoma. She has just arrived after a three-day trip from Anchorage, Alaska, and will turn around in less than twelve hours to make another journey to the Last Frontier with another load of cargo.

| Photo by **Alan S. Weiner**|

TOTE Can Carry the Load from Tacoma to Anchorage

Every week, two Orca Class vessels, the *M.V. Midnight Sun* and the *M.V. North Star*, leave the Port of Tacoma and begin the three-day journey to Anchorage, Alaska. The vessels depart on Thursday and Saturday mornings. The ships safely carry everything from household goods and food to automobiles and construction equipment. Upon arrival, their northbound cargo is unloaded, and southbound freight is brought aboard. The ships then return to Tacoma. Their routine is as reliable as the rising and setting sun. And that dependability is the hallmark of Totem Ocean Trailer Express, Inc. (TOTE).

Established in 1975 when Philadelphia's Sun Company launched a roll-on/roll-off (Ro/Ro) steamship venture in Seattle (the company relocated to Tacoma in 1976), TOTE has become the premier provider of ocean transportation service to Alaska. The privately owned company began with one Ponce Class vessel, the *S.S. Great Land*, but quickly grew its fleet and repertoire of services after being purchased by Totem Resources Corporation in 1982. Today, TOTE not only provides exceptional Ro/Ro cargo ship service between the Port of Tacoma and the Port of Anchorage, but also provides full trailer load shipping and Logistics Service between road-connected Alaska and the lower forty-eight states and Canada.

At the heart of TOTE's business is the desire to exceed customers' expectations. That's why the company invested more than $400 million in the construction of its newest Orca Class vessels, which can carry fifty-three-foot and larger-length trailers, provide dedicated vehicle stowage for automobile shippers, and more. The state-of-the-art ships, crewed by highly trained merchant mariners, are specifically designed for the rigors of Alaskan trade, and their Ro/Ro capabilities allow cargo to be driven onto and off of the vessels quickly and easily by special tractors, eliminating the costs and time associated with transloading.

Additionally, from their engines to their structures, the vessels surpass environmental regulations.

Additionally, from their engines to their structures, the vessels surpass environmental regulations, with marine safety features like double hulls, vertical fuel tanks, and completely contained ballast water. TOTE received the U.S. Coast Guard Biennial William M. Benkert Foundation 2002 Environmental Excellence Bronze Award for the ships' design, among other honors. And because the company's environmentally conscious efforts extend to everything it does, TOTE earned Washington's 2005 Governor's Award for Pollution Prevention & Sustainable Practices.

For TOTE, showing concern for the environment is just one aspect of being a good corporate citizen. As a proud member of the Tacoma and Anchorage communities, the company also donates thousands of dollars and in-kind contributions to local charities and is involved in a variety of philanthropic activities for education, youth-oriented, maritime, and nonprofit organizations. TOTE also dedicates itself to litter prevention and environmental efforts in Alaska. The reason is simple. At TOTE, demonstrating civic leadership and environmental responsibility is just as important as operating a profitable business.

In the future, TOTE will continue to strategically invest in and improve its operations so it can provide the best service possible. Customers from across the lower forty-eight to Alaska can depend on it. ■

Port engineer Mike Patrick keeps a watchful eye on the unloading and loading of this Ro/Ro cargo ship, docked alongside the TOTE terminal in the Port of Tacoma.

| Photo by **Jackson Hill** |

From the first cargo of tea, which arrived in 1885, just one year after Tacoma was officially established, the city has enjoyed an Asian influence. Today visitors and residents alike can enjoy the flavors of Asia at the Indochine Asian Dining Lounge conveniently located near the University of Washington's Pacific Avenue campus. It took twenty months of careful planning and construction to accomplish the vision of the Ngov family, who own two other restaurants in town. The original location is located on Federal Way and the second one in Fircrest. The décor and the menu of Indochine reflect the tastes of Thailand, China, Japan, and India. Exotic lacquered woods, black leather, a table-side fountain and pool, and a back bar that changes colors make this truly a fusion of upscale Asian cuisine and American high-tech design. "The Ngov family has been in the restaurant business here for more than fifteen years, and opening a location downtown seemed the right move since lots of our customers live in Pierce County," said Russel Brunton, co-owner. ■

| Photo by **Jackson Hill** |

| Photo by **Jackson Hill** |

Thea's Landing is a project whose master plan calls for a mix of residential, commercial, recreational, and entertainment facilities. Located on the eastern edge of downtown Tacoma, the Thea Foss Waterway Development Authority is guiding the redevelopment of twenty-seven acres of city-owned property along a one-and-a-half-mile stretch of the Foss Waterway. The project was developed by an all-local group that "wanted to put something there that we'd be proud of for the rest of our lives," said Kim Nakamura, one of the six partners in the project. The first anchor to move in was the Museum of Glass, and other businesses followed, among them the Blue Olive Restaurant. Shades of blue in the room match a number of the martinis on the menu. But it is the bar that makes this restaurant super cool: a trough of ice runs its entire length. The view isn't bad either, looking out onto the Thea Foss Waterway, the Museum of Glass, the International Center for Contemporary Art, and, of course, Mount Rainier. ■

LeMay Transportation
Division supervisor Larry Meany and drivers Roger Bratsch, Mitch Hensell, and Jesus Corona are part of the force that keeps the trucks on the road. LeMay provides heavy-haul tractor-trailer service, single- and double-drop truck service, and heavy-haul dump truck and pup service to customers throughout Washington, northern Idaho, and northern Oregon. Their shredding trucks can destroy documents containing federally protected information in the financial, medical, and legal fields while the customer watches.

| Photo by **Jackson Hill** |

LeMay Enterprises, Inc.–Offering Generations of Service

South Pierce County native Harold LeMay was an original energetic multi-tasker. In the early 1940s, he drove workers to and from the Tacoma shipyards in what was then called a "Victory Bus." He also hauled scrap metal, wood, and furniture and, seeing a need to haul garbage in the Spanaway-Parkland area, took a 1935 Chevrolet from his hauling business and converted it into a garbage truck. He obtained a permit, and Harold E. LeMay was on his way to building what would become a major business in the Pierce County area. Harold's friends laughed at him, thinking that taking a truck from a good-paying job and putting a wooden box with a hand-crank dump to haul garbage was foolish. He proved them wrong by not only becoming a successful garbage hauler in South Pierce County, but also throughout the State of Washington. Through the years, as the business evolved into the successful entity it is now, Harold was heavily involved in the community and became a beloved local figure.

> *"Service is the only commodity we have, so we really emphasize friendly service to all our customers. It's what we've built our reputation on."*

Currently, LeMay Enterprises is one of the largest and one of the few remaining family-owned refuse companies in the United States. Their total collection area extends from Mount Rainier to the ocean and from Puget Sound to the Cowlitz River with approximately 160,000 customers. The LeMay family not only owns the company, but is also involved in its day-to-day operation. Nancy LeMay is president, Norm is in charge of contracts and operations, Hal takes care of property management, Doug supervises maintenance of trucks and equipment, and Barbara is corporate secretary.

"I believe we continue to be successful because we understand that service always comes first. Conscientious waste removal and recycling are at the forefront of what ecology is all about, and we're aware that we provide an essential service for our community," said Norm.

Nancy agrees. "Service is the only commodity we have, so we really emphasize friendly service to all our customers. It's what we've built our reputation on." Friendly service was what Harold expected from his employees.

In response to customers' needs, document destruction has become a fast-growing segment of the business. "Since identity theft has become such an issue, businesses that handle personal information must guarantee the information is destroyed beyond recognition. This is especially true with medical records, banking information, and any establishment that handles credit card or Social Security identification," Norm explained. Specially equipped LeMay Shredding trucks were purchased by the company in response to new privacy laws. These trucks are able to destroy sensitive documents and other media on-site while the customer watches. That material is then recycled, and a crucial service is provided to the community..

For the past sixty years, LeMay has been serving communities through its business, and it also serves in other ways. "We're all very active in local and state organizations," Nancy said. "We serve on boards, and we keep an eye on the communities. When there's a need, we try to jump in and help." This philosophy is evident by the contributions LeMay has made locally, such as the Harold LeMay Car Museum and the Harold

| Continued on page 126 |

South Pierce County businessman Harold LeMay would be proud to see that his family is carrying on the business he started in the early 1940s. Today LeMay Enterprises is one of the largest and one of the few remaining family-owned refuse companies in the United States. Actively involved in keeping the family tradition alive are members of the Board of Directors Hal LeMay, Doug LeMay, Barb LeMay-Quinn, Debbie LeMay-Shepherd, Dixie LeMay-Marien, Nancy LeMay, Norm LeMay, and Scott Penner.

There has been a big change in the equipment since Harold LeMay took a 1935 Chevrolet from his hauling business and converted it into a garbage truck. From that simple beginning, he created what would become a major business in the Pierce County area and throughout Washington state. Today Dan Egnew, Ric Thompson, Doug LeMay, and Norm LeMay (left to right) are busy in LeMay Enterprises Tacoma Disposal Division.

| Photo by **Jackson Hill** |

| Continued from page 125 |

E. LeMay Skateboard Park. They are evident in other ways too, whether it's participating in local parades where dignitaries ride in "LeMay cars," sponsoring children's sport teams, or supporting many charitable causes. The company also places great emphasis on being a caring employer, and staff retention demonstrates this. Many current and retired employees have worked a lifetime for the company, and some of the retirees now volunteer their time to the museum. The LeMay family continues to run their business with dedication to service excellence, diligent concern for the environment, and involvement in the community. ■

Nancy LeMay and her grandchildren Stewart LeMay, Cody LeMay Marien, Justin LeMay (in helmet), Adam LeMay, and Jordin LeMay Quinn are standing in the largest all-concrete skateboard park in Washington. Built through the fund-raising efforts of Nancy's Altrusa Club, the Skate Park encouraged local skaters of all ages to participate in its design. The park has skate features for beginning, intermediate, and advanced skaters and multiple shade structures and bleachers for families and guests who just come to watch.

| Photo by **Jackson Hill** |

| Photo by **Eric Francis** |

One of the most popular attractions at Sprinker Recreation Center is the Harold E. LeMay Skate Park, which was developed in cooperation with the Washington Wildlife and Recreation Program through a $275,000 grant from the Interagency Committee for Outdoor Recreation and matching local donations of $100,000 from Nancy LeMay, plus donations from Altrusa Foundation and Pierce County. The facility is the largest all-concrete skateboard parks in Washington. Its twenty-seven thousand square feet include specialized features to accommodate everyone from beginners to advanced skateboarders and in-line skaters. Sprinker Recreation Center also includes an a full-sized ice arena, indoor and outdoor tennis courts, and several softball fields, which make year-round recreation and classes available.

When she was eight years old, Whitney Conder had a dream. Endless miles of roadwork, countless hours on the mat, and diligent training in the weight room paid off, and as a Puyallup High School senior, she realized her dream. Whitney Conder is a championship wrestler, a female wrestler, competing against boys. She joined a wrestling club at eight, and two years later, her father started the Puyallup Falcons. Initially, her family thought it was just a whim. Not anymore. "She's a very hard worker," said Puyallup coach Brian Bartelson, "and she's a great wrestler, gender aside." Her passion and dedication to the sport earned her team captain status and a reputation with her fellow wrestlers. "I learned everything from my father and two older brothers. Dustin and Nate. They both wrestled at Rogers High School, and my dad wrestled in both high school and college." Whitney's wins qualified her for the United States National Team, which competes internationally. Her goal is to compete in the Olympics, and at the rate she's going, there is every good chance she will realize that ambition. ∎

| Photo by **Jim Bryant** |

The Thea Foss Waterway bustles with recreational boating activity—in everything from elegant yachts to streamlined kayaks. Paddlers can put in at any number of places in and around the Sound, with popular routes including the four-mile round-trip from Commencement Park into the Thea Foss Waterway. Additional launch points into scenic routes are at Point Defiance Park and Ruston Way. Those new to the area can get a good feel for paddling opportunities by joining one of the area's numerous padding clubs. These range from recreational organizations like the Gig Harbor Kayak Club to amateur athletic clubs with races and fun runs, such as the Tacoma Dragon Boat Association. ■

| Photo by **Alan S. Weiner** |

The World Trade Center Tacoma provides its members with the resources they need to succeed in international trade and investment. The organization knows that connecting people the old-fashioned way is the basis to good business around the world.

World Trade Center Tacoma Focuses on Connecting People

In the global marketplace, the right relationships can mean all the difference. Helping companies make the most rewarding international connections is the World Trade Center Tacoma.

As an organization focused on the human interaction that is the basis of good business, the World Trade Center Tacoma works with its members to build the confidence and skills they need to do business in a global economy. By combining resources such as training, counseling, referrals, and market intelligence with a real back-to-the-basics approach to business, the organization equips its members to succeed in their overseas trade and investment endeavors.

> *The World Trade Center Tacoma works with its members to build the confidence and skills they need to do business in a global economy.*

In addition, as part of an international system of world trade centers, the World Trade Center Tacoma also offers its members unlimited global networking opportunities. This worldwide connection brings to the table a host of leads and contacts that are so vital to success when negotiating and selling abroad.

Through its training programs, the organization offers its members a wealth of learning opportunities.

Licensed by the Port of Tacoma, the World Trade Center Tacoma has been centered for more than a quarter-century on bringing the region global recognition and increased trade. This emphasis over the years has helped to produce new jobs, a larger tax base, and overall economic growth for the state and its people.

Washington companies have a lot to offer the world's people, and when they want to trade around the globe, their best partner can be found at the World Trade Center Tacoma. ■

| Photo by **Alan S. Weiner** |

| Photo by **Jim Bryant** |

When Fort Nisqually, a Hudson's Bay Company outpost, was established back in 1833, Tacoma was on the cusp of a new era. The fur trade, which was beginning to boom, would soon make an indelible mark on the maritime industry of the Northwest. In 1855, the upsurge made its way to Washington State and the first European settlement on Puget Sound, with hundreds of traders bringing their horses, laden with furs, to Fort Nisqually from the interior of the Northwest. Today, that momentous event is re-created annually during the Fort Nisqually Brigade Encampment. During the two-day affair, more than one hundred reenactors step back in time to 1855, bringing the past to life for attendees so they can see firsthand what happened when the fur brigades arrived in the Washington Territory. The family-friendly event also features a wide range of entertainment options, from Fur Trappers' Races and ladies' teas to hands-on presentations like fire starting with flint and steel, blacksmithing, and spinning wool. All the while, the sounds of bagpipes fill the air, just like they did in bygone days. And all visitors have to do to journey to the mid-nineteenth century is take a short trip to Point Defiance Park, where the Fort Nisqually Living History Museum is located. ■

| Photo by **Jim Bryant** |

Rich in History

| Photo by **Jackson Hill** |

Makes sense that the building used to house the relics that chronicle the Evergreen State's evolution is just as awesome and engaging. Located on Pacific Avenue in Tacoma, the Washington State History Museum offers more than one hundred thousand square feet of spectacular exhibit space, designed by renowned architects Charles Moore and Arthur Andersson. This is where Washington's saga unfolds for visitors young and old. From the Great Hall of Washington History to the Model Railroad, an impressive collection of three-dimensional, interactive, and high-tech displays let day-trippers explore coalmines like William Clark did, journey down the Columbia River, work on the railroad from Point Defiance Park to the Stampede Pass Tunnel, ride in a covered wagon, and more. There's even a History Lab Learning Center, where students can explore history hands-on, researching and solving historical mysteries using the Tools of the History Trade, including pictures, books, and oral histories. Operated by the Washington State Historical Society, the museum is an ever-growing resource that undoubtedly will keep the state's history alive for generations to come. ■

The Tacoma–Pierce County Chamber's twenty-fifth annual Howard O. Scott Citizen-Soldier of the Year award for exemplary community volunteerism is given to McChord Air Force Base's citizen-airman Master Sergeant Theron Smith, by sponsor Tri West HealthCare Alliance.

| Photo by **Jim Bryant** |

TPCC Aims to Promote and Build Local Businesses

With a keen understanding that a city's economic prosperity and quality of life are inextricably connected, the Tacoma–Pierce County Chamber of Commerce's top priorities are to build, sustain, and promote the area's business environment. "We accomplish this through advocacy, networking, resources, and business development services," says president and CEO David Graybill. "There truly is power through connections."

The Tacoma–Pierce County Chamber of Commerce (TPCC) takes to the highest of levels its role as the single most powerful advocacy group for businesses. As a result, the United States Chamber of Commerce has awarded TPCC an elite five-star accreditation, which is "one of the highest honors bestowed on local chambers fighting for pro-growth and jobs policies," according to the U.S. Chamber of Commerce president. In other words, TPCC is recognized among its peer organizations as consistently being a chamber that offers values to both its

While there is indeed "power through connections," there is also power in information.

members and its community. For example, the Chamber has provided an unwavering commitment to advocacy at all levels—local, state, and federal—on behalf of all area businesses and military installations, including the Northwest's longest-running annual civic leaders' trip to Washington, D.C. "These efforts ensure that principal issues, such as health care, education, and transportation, as well as tax and regulatory competitiveness, remain a top priority with government officials," says Graybill. "We're making sure they understand the Pierce County business community, and more importantly, that they get all the information they need to make sound decisions."

While there is indeed "power through connections," there is also power in information. "Businesses live and die in the local economy. Assessing the health of the economy is critical to daily business and, as such, is an important objective of ours," he says. The Pierce County Economic Index (PCEI), originated by the Chamber and prepared annually by University of Puget Sound professors of economics, is one of only a few econometric models in the nation providing a consistent local economic index. Graybill calls the PCEI both an affirming and confirming document. Members call it indispensable. Key factors are consistently tracked, which is helpful for business forecasting.

Being a member of the TPCC creates important connections and provides opportunities to receive helpful products, participate in special programs, and join area leadership in actions that enable companies, individuals, and, as a result, the region to do and achieve more. "Tacoma is a community filled with continuous promise, revitalization, and economic development," says Graybill. "Businesses are enthusiastic about our community, and about our Chamber, and we are too. Together, we'll continue to advance Tacoma–Pierce County as 'One of America's Most Livable Communities.'" ■

The Tacoma–Pierce County Chamber Annual Meeting draws a large crowd as members representing the breadth of the area's business community gather for a thought-provoking address by notable creative economist, Dr. Richard Florida. During its numerous events each year, the Chamber strives to present similar high-profile speakers who bring ideas and action plans to assist area leadership in keeping Tacoma–Pierce County on the cutting edge of economic development. Since 1884, the Tacoma–Pierce County Chamber's strategic focus has been on providing economic opportunity and a more livable community.

| Photo by **Eric Francis** |

| Photo by **Eric Francis** |

Picking the perfect pumpkin is a ritual of fall that is one part skill and the other part pleasure. Hmmmmm, let's see. . . . Should it be stout or tall? A prominent stem? How large? Will its surface imperfections be carved away, or left bare to honor its natural state? With fall colors as the backdrop, a pumpkin patch like the one at Ken M. Spooner Farm off State Road 162 East in Puyallup offers a real treat for the senses. Pumpkin pickers of all ages can touch and see the objects of their search, as the scent of a crisp autumn day gently reminds them that the season of the harvest is also the season of gratitude. ■

For nearly sixty years, Tacoma has welcomed Santa and the holiday season with a parade and the lighting of the city's official Christmas tree. The parade starts in the Stadium District—one of Tacoma's twelve neighborhood business districts—and proceeds downtown to Ninth and Broadway. Along with floats, marching bands, vintage autos, and bundled-up spectators, the holiday season would not be complete without the donation each year by Fort Lewis of a gigantic tree. It is a tradition that started in 1946. It is their way of recognizing the Tacoma community's continued support of the armed forces. ■

The annual Festival of Trees is a Tacoma tradition that brings delight to hundreds of children and adults each year during the holidays. However, the benefits of this event are felt long after the trees have been removed from the Greater Tacoma Convention & Trade Center. Funds go to support the Mary Bridge Children's Hospital, founded by local physician A. W. Bridge, who passed away in 1947. He left his large estate to be used to help start a children's hospital and requested that it be named for his mother, Mary. The hospital first opened in 1955. Today, Mary Bridge Children's Hospital & Health Center is the only pediatric hospital in southwest Washington dedicated to care for the special health needs of children. ■

Celebrate the Seasons

If breakfast is the most important way to start the day, then a relaxing after-dinner drink is a great way to end it. The hotel's lobby lounge serves on-tap and bottled beer, domestic and imported wines, and a wide selection of liquors and aperitifs.

| Photo by **Eric Francis** |

Courtyard by Marriott Offers the Ultimate in Guest Experience

As one of the city's best full-service hotels, the Courtyard by Marriott–Tacoma Downtown bears all the distinctive touches long associated with the Marriott name. Whether a guest is traveling for business or pleasure, the hotel's warm service, modern conveniences, and centralized location combine to create nothing less than the ultimate lodging experience.

Accommodations include 162 rooms featuring the best in comfort and convenience, from luxury bedding to a work desk and chair to free high-speed Internet. All of the rooms also offer guests microwaves and refrigerators, sofa beds, and expanded phone service including voice mail, two lines, and speakerphone.

With forty-three hundred square feet of ballroom/meeting space that seats up to 250 guests, the Courtyard is a favorite for special events like weddings and family parties. The ballroom may also be divided into smaller rooms, which makes it a comfortable area for meetings, luncheons, and other business events. Situated directly across the street from the Greater Tacoma Convention and Trade Center, and within a short walk's distance of the city's light rail transportation system, the hotel is a favorite with conventioneers.

Making guests feel special and at home has been the mission of the Marriott family of hotels for over seventy-five years.

Pleasure travelers also appreciate the Courtyard's amenities and convenient location. After a day of sightseeing, guests can relax with a swim in the hotel's indoor pool, a soothing massage at the luxurious day spa, or even a quick jog on the treadmill at the fitness center. And from its location in the heart of downtown Tacoma, guests have easy access to miles of walking and bicycling trails, golf, several walking tours, and many first class museums such as The Washington State History Museum, The International Museum of Glass and Contemporary Art, The Tacoma Art Museum and The Chihuly Bridge of Glass.

| Continued on page 140 |

With its grand staircase, elegant lobby, and friendly staff, the hotel makes visitors feel right at home from the start.

| Photo by **Alan S. Weiner** |

| Photo by **Eric Francis** |

Visitors who are in town for large gatherings like weddings, reunions, or anniversaries appreciate the Marriott's many thoughtful touches. The hotel's library, for instance, provides a comfortable, cozy, and private gathering place for friends and family.

| Continued from page 138 |

Those who want to dine in have a lunch and dinner option at the Pacific Grill or by ordering evening room service. For breakfast, the Courtyard Café serves American-style breakfast favorites from both a menu and sumptuous buffet.

Making guests feel special and at home has been the mission of the Marriott family of hotels for over seventy-five years. As part of this family, the Courtyard by Marriott–Tacoma Downtown works to provide guests with nothing less than the best that Marriott and Tacoma have to offer. ■

There's plenty of room to stretch out and relax in a Marriott room. And with each bed featuring down pillows, luxury bedding, and top-quality mattresses, a good night's sleep is virtually guaranteed.

| Photo by **Eric Francis** |

A job like this takes a cool head, steady hands, and an immunity to heights that not many of us possess. But think of the views! They are certainly a major perk for the people tasked with keeping squeaky clean the hundreds of panels of glass that make up the Greater Tacoma Convention and Trade Center. Located at South fifteenth and Commerce streets just south of the business district, the soaring, glass-walled facility was designed to provide wraparound views of the city and its surroundings while at the same time encouraging interaction between the outside and inside environments. A fully equipped, high-tech center with nearly 125,000 square feet of meeting and event space, GTCTC is also conveniently situated within walking distance of some of the city's best hotels, restaurants, art galleries, and specialty shops. ■

| Photo by **Eric Francis** |

BAIR DRUG & HARDWARE

OPEN

| Photo by **Eric Francis** |

Every town needs a place that serves up heaping helpings of old-fashioned food and drink, along with a relaxed and cozy atmosphere that bans cell phones and encourages lively conversations. In Steilacoom that place is the Bair Restaurant and Catering. The historic 1895 building once housed the town's drug and hardware store, its post office, and during the 1970s Jeff "The Frugal Gourmet" Smith's coffeeshop. The restaurant's owners, Ed and Martha Lintott, lease the building's front room from the Steilacoom Historical Museum Association and help fulfill the organization's mission to preserve it as a living museum. The Bair's dining room is decorated with historic artifacts, including the original soda fountain. But the food and drink are the Lintotts' own, made fresh daily from available local ingredients. Known for their breakfasts, including a splendid seafood Eggs Benedict and what some call the best French toast in Washington, the Bair also serves terrific soups, salads, and sandwiches for lunch and dinnertime fare that ranges from comforting (try the fried chicken) to creative, like crawfish-stuffed pork chops and steak with Roquefort dressing. And since Ed is trained as a baker, you know the desserts are to die for. ■

N ow that it has become so much a part of the downtown culture, it may be hard to remember that the idea of renovating warehouses to create a new University of Washington branch campus was not a slam-dunk. The mayor at the time, Bill Baarsma, however, recalls that he thought it was a stroke of genius . . . and so it has turned out to be. When it opened in 2002, the campus served approximately two thousand juniors, seniors, and graduate students. The location is easily accessible by car and offers a plot of land that will eventually expand to accommodate up to twenty thousand students. A local landscape firm, Bruce Dees & Associates, has been involved in the master planning and all development phases to date, including pedestrian walkways, plazas, and planting. Care was taken to preserve the industrial character of the Warehouse District. BD&A worked directly with the project architects to incorporate new and old buildings into the campus and to once again bring life and excitement to a historic Tacoma landmark. ■

At the heart of downtown Tacoma's revitalization is KeyBank Plaza, a one-hundred-year-old building brought back to life as part of the bank's investment in a vital city.

KeyBank Strives to Give Back to Community through Service

More than anything else, KeyBank is all about building things in Tacoma and Pierce County. Helping families build their futures and helping businesses grow. Building careers for its staff. And building community to make our region's quality of life more fulfilling.

The philosophy Key brings to this community is a simple one, but not one every business shares: This community is very good to the bank, and Key's responsibility is to give back, both through its products and services and by being a good neighbor.

> *"To be successful over the long term, the bank and the community must be mutually supportive of each other, and that's the way it is here."*

"To be successful over the long term," says Thomas Spilman, president of Key's South Puget Sound District, "the bank and the community must be mutually supportive of each other, and that's the way it is here."

KeyBank came to Tacoma in 1993. Its entry into this vibrant market was similar to its entry into other markets all across the northern tier of states, from Maine to Alaska. It acquired an existing local financial institution, added strength and staff—and many new ways to serve the local community.

Strategically woven together in the state and nationally, Key's franchise encompasses most of western and central Washington. So, whether a customer's need is national or in the Northwest, Key can help.

| Photo by **Jim Bryant** |

One longtime local customer of Key is Puyallup-based Korum Automotive Group, a leading retailer of Ford, Hyundai, and Mitsubishi vehicles that has experience with Key and its local predecessor banks dating back to 1956.

CEO Jerry Korum says, "Key brought new strengths to this market and to our business. The bank offered a worldview that was right for the growth and change we were experiencing in the auto business, and which helped us remain competitive."

Most importantly, Korum adds, "Key got to know us. The bank logo changed, but that was about all. The bank integrated its culture with ours."

As the relationship has matured through the years, Key today handles Korum's financing, checking, depository, trusts, and real estate.

Korum lauds Key equally for its commitment to the local communities of Pierce County. "Pick most any charitable cause in our area, and it's been touched in a significant way by KeyBank," Korum says.

Key's Spilman is proud that Key is involved in the community on several levels. Philanthropy is important, but it is far from the only thing Key does. "I think it is critical that Key's staff be person- ally involved in the community. Giving back comes from the heart even more than the checkbook," he says.

A centerpiece of that human involvement is Key's "Neighbors Make a Difference Day." One day each fall, most of its KeyCenters, as well as the administrative offices, close so that the staff can fan out and make a real impact. Over the years, Key workers have

| Continued on page 146 |

| Photo by **Jackson Hill** |

One day each year, on Neighbors Make a Difference Day, the field of banking takes on new meaning as KeyBank staff donate their time to making our communities a better place to live.

One of the region's top civic boosters and business leaders, automobile dealer Jerry Korum remains one of Key's most loyal clients.

| Continued from page 145 |

given fresh coats of paint to day-care centers and helped repair senior centers. They have picked up litter on public beaches and taken on projects at schools.

"Having five hundred individuals giving their time really makes a difference right here in Pierce County," Spilman notes. "You cannot believe the camaraderie it creates among our employees."

Another annual commitment grew from the need to support the revival of downtown Tacoma. Things were happening, but the team at Key felt the bank could take on its own signature event.

In 2000, the bank partnered with the City of Tacoma to launch a running event from the center of downtown to Commencement Bay: Bank to Bay. In just its first few years, the event expanded from hundreds of participants to thousands. It now includes health and wellness activities, food, and music, and it's become an event on everyone's calendar here.

| Photo by **Jackson Hill** |

Bank to Bay supports the Tacoma Public Schools Help-a-Student Fund, which provides necessities such as school supplies, clothing, and shoes to local students in need. Through the lead participation of KeyBank and the support of many other organizations, Bank to Bay donated sixty thousand dollars to the Fund in just its first six years.

Key's contributions support many aspects of the community, such as the creation of the KeyBank Professional Development Center. It's a joint venture involving the bank, the Dimmer Family Foundation, and the University of Washington–Tacoma campus to extend the resources of the university to our community. The Center works with educational providers to offer a broad array of continuing education opportunities for public- and private-sector professionals and organizations in a range of disciplines.

Spilman is proud of the leadership role the bank has assumed in Tacoma and Pierce County.

Affordable housing for
seniors is a priority in Pierce County and at KeyBank. Puyallup's Sunset Garden received financing from Key to help make it a reality.

| Photo by **Jim Bryant** |

They're off!
One of the favorite events of the annual Bank to Bay is the 1K Kids' Run, presented by KeyBank and the City of Tacoma.

"The formula we subscribe to is pretty simple," he says. "We are part of a thriving community, and we bring energy and resources to help build it into an even better place. And a vital, successful community is clearly better for us as well." ■

A need for continuing education for professionals drove KeyBank and the Dimmer Family Foundation to launch the KeyBank Professional Development Center at UW-Tacoma. From left to right, Key's Tom Spilman, the Center's director Alice Dionne, and Chancellor Patricia Spakes.

| Photo by **Alan S. Weiner** |

It's no surprise that the impressive woodcarving Karen Pollak is painting here looks so realistic—she's been working on it for months as one of Larry Martin's students. An avid woodcarver for many years, Martin offers classes in his home studio a couple of times a week for individuals who want to learn the fine art of bird carving. He picked up the craft himself when his wife gave him a gift of lessons with a local master bird carver. Now, he revels in the opportunity not only to whittle pieces of wood into beautiful and lifelike sculptures, but also to research his subjects thoroughly, doing everything from birdwatching to taking photos of his favorite feathered friends in their natural habitats for reference. He often draws the patterns he uses and enjoys seeing his visions come to fruition. "What really intrigues me is taking a two-dimensional, flat diagram and making it into a three-dimensional piece," he says. "It's just wonderful watching it all come together." Novice woodcarvers agree and are lining up to learn from one of the best: there's actually a waiting list to become a student in one of his small, intimate classes.

| Photo by **Jackson Hill** |

| Photo by **Jackson Hill** |

Dave Robertson, the founder and president of Gig Harbor Boat Works, has enjoyed building things since he was thirteen and constructed his first boat. In 1977, Dave and his wife, Janet, bought an unfinished Mercator 30 and made a beautiful cruiser out of it. However, they couldn't find a proper dinghy to complete the traditional look, so they built one. They have been building graceful rowboats and day-sailors ever since, producing approximately one hundred boats a year, by hand, one at a time. "Customers can order anything from a basic utility version to our exclusive limited edition with gold-plated hardware," said Dave. "Most boats are designed for one purpose only. In all our designs, we strive for maximum versatility, simplicity, and efficiency. Our boats can be rowed, towed, stowed, and sailed." Gig Harbor Boats takes most of its orders in January during the Seattle Boat Show, so if you want one, get your order in early. ■

| Photo by **Jim Bryant** |

The Tacoma Farmers Market was established not only to offer customers farm-fresh produce, but also to create something beautiful out of something blighted. When Tacoma residents Marcia Moe and Norma Honeysett walked through the city's downtown in 1990, they saw deserted streets strewn with debris. What they envisioned was something else entirely: a place that would help revitalize the area and bring with it a renewed sense of community. When their farmers market opened on its first day in the summer of 1990, forty vendors showed up to sell. Today, the Tacoma Farmers Market has grown to include two locations and one hundred vendors representing the finest farmers, crafters, and food processors in Washington State. Tiny's Organic Farm, which has been selling at the Broadway market since 2002, is known for its fresh stone fruits like peaches, plums, nectarines, and cherries, plus two specialty fruits—the donut peach and the pluot, a plum/apricot hybrid. ■

| Photo by **Jim Bryant** |

There's something beautiful to discover at every turn during a stroll through the W. W. Seymour Botanical Conservatory. Located in Wright Park, the historic conservatory features a twelve-sided central dome; thirty-five hundred panes of glass; and over five hundred plant species, two hundred different orchids, and up to five hundred blooming plants depending on the time of year. Open year-round, Tuesdays through Sundays, the conservatory offers both guided and self-guided tours. It also hosts several yearly plant sales, a monthly concert series, a Halloween event at its pumpkin patch, and a Victorian Christmas celebration that benefits the Tacoma Rescue Mission Family Shelter. ■

| Photo by **Eric Francis** |

| Photo by **Eric Francis** |

This building in Tacoma is both the downtown branch and corporate headquarters for Sound Credit Union. The company was founded as Telco Community Credit Union in 1940 by fifty-one employees of Pacific Telephone and Telegraph with total operating deposits of $106.50. Today Sound Credit Union has assets exceeding $300 million and ten branch locations, and offers a full range of financial services to customers throughout the Tacoma area.

| Photo by **Alan S. Weiner** |

Sound Credit Union Aims to Delight its Members

How would you like to know someone whose job was to delight you? If you were a member of Sound Credit Union—and you can be if you live or work in Washington state—you would have just that.

"We recently conducted a survey and found the top priority with our members was to make things easier, faster, and more convenient, so we're realigning our strategy to look for ways to delight our members," said Rick Brandsma, president and CEO.

For instance, Sound Credit Union introduced digital signature pads, which eliminate the necessity of multiple signatures on loan applications. New online services, which eliminate multiple face-to-face meetings, also streamline the process. Two new branch offices offer added convenience.

"Our members know we'll look out for their best interests and educate them so they make good, long-term decisions," Brandsma continued. The trust built between SCU and members begins on their first visit. "We sit down with them and analyze ways they can save money. It might be by transferring high-interest credit card totals to our lower-interest cards, or by financing their cars through us."

> *"Our members know we'll look out for their best interests and educate them so they make good, long-term decisions."*

Perhaps a word here should be said about the difference between a bank and a credit union. The main difference is that Sound Credit Union is not-for-profit. That means each person who opens an account becomes a member, or stakeholder, with a vote. "Unlike a bank, whose responsibility is to pay dividends to its stockholders, our responsibility is to offer competitive rates and more specialized services to our members," said Brandsma.

An important SCU service—that hopefully members will never need—is a well-thought-out and rehearsed plan to deal with a potential disaster. "We have a backup generator so we can continue to give service from our main office in any event where we lose power. We've also contracted a nationally recognized company to provide backup data processing, should we lose data processing capabilities. Through 'hot sites' located throughout the country, we can reestablish processing as early as twenty-four hours following a catastrophe."

On a lighter note, SCU also actively supports its communities. Each year SCU offers scholarships to graduating high school seniors who plan to attend a two- or four-year college. They also sponsor a number of employee activities to raise money for United Way, the American Cancer Society, and the March of Dimes. "On Fridays, we allow employees who donate five dollars to the designated cause to wear jeans. Twice a year we hold an internal online auction, where each department creates a theme basket and they're auctioned, similar to eBay. We've had coffee baskets, sports tickets, family game baskets, and movie baskets. It's fun and for a good cause," said Brandsma.

Make it fast, easy, convenient, and have fun doing it. That is the Sound Credit Union way. ■

For over sixty years, Sound Credit Union has been part of the growth and development of Tacoma. Today Sound Credit Union shares the downtown neighborhood with historic buildings like Union Station, which was resurrected as the United States Federal Courthouse.

| Photo by **Alan S. Weiner** |

Carved out of the ravine next to the school in 1909, the Bowl has been the site of football games, marching band competitions, historical reenactments, presidential speeches, and a host of performances by personalities such as John Philip Sousa and Louis Armstrong. Although the Bowl has been plagued with architectural challenges over the years, its advocates have successfully argued for a number of renovations that have kept it intact and a source of pride for the community. ■

| Photo by **David Gibb** |

When construction first began in 1891 on the building that would become Stadium High School, financiers of the project thought they were erecting one of the finest hotels on the West Coast. But the financial panic of 1893 left the French Renaissance–style structure unfinished, and its owners decided to dismantle the structure and cart the bricks off to other destinations for use in building train depots. That's when local leaders stepped in to secure the "castle" for its current use as one of seven high schools in the Tacoma Public School District. Beyond a core curriculum, the school offers both visual and performing arts studies, vocational education opportunities, athletics, and social and leadership activities. ■

| Photo by **David Gibb** |

Whether you are visiting Point Defiance Park, Point Defiance Zoo and Aquarium, Ruston Way, Tacoma Nature Center, the W. W. Seymour Botanical Conservatory, the off-leash dog area at Rogers Park, Northwest Trek, or Greenhouse, Tacoma city parks offer something for everyone. Metro Parks Tacoma has its roots in the City of Tacoma Charter of 1880 and was incorporated April 6, 1907. Tacoma resident Colonel Clinton Ferry gave the city its first space, and Ferry Park was dedicated in 1883. Five years later, Tacoma persuaded Congress to allow park development at Point Defiance, and in 1905 Congress granted the city full title to the 638-acre park. For more than one hundred years Metro Parks Tacoma has continued to maintain and care for Tacoma's park resources. Since 2001, Parks Appreciation Day has given residents a chance to participate in a countywide event to spruce up, fix up, and plant new flowers in the parks. So far, nearly three thousand volunteers have donated over ten thousand hours to the cause. ■

The Tacoma branch of the Karpeles Manuscript Museums is part of a unique museum collection. In all, there are eight museums scattered throughout the country. The archives include an astonishing collection of original manuscripts ranging from musical scores by Beethoven, to ancient Papyrus texts, to the cover letter for the Declaration of Independence and the decoded instructions to negotiate for the independence of the United States by Benjamin Franklin. "There are no permanent collections," said Tom Jutilla, director of the local branch. "Rotating manuscripts change every three months. It's heart-stopping each time I open a new collection and see what's there. And perhaps the best part is that admission to all the museums is free and available to the public." The founder, David Karpeles, is a real estate magnate from Santa Barbara. All the buildings are in "intensive-care neighborhoods" because Karpeles wants to give people who wouldn't normally have exposure to museums a chance to visit. ■

| Photo by **Jackson Hill** |

| Photo by **Jackson Hill** |

At the time of his death in 2000, Harold LeMay had assembled the world's largest private car collection. Estimates placed the number of cars at nearly twenty-five hundred. "The cars were an excuse to make new friends and for old friends to get together," said grandson Eric. LeMay's widow, Nancy, often greets guests at the Harold LeMay Museum. "Harold loved his family, his friends, America, and anything on wheels," she said. The museum includes cars long gone like Hupmobiles, Hudsons, Humbers, Marmons, Edsels, and a Briscoe that had one headlight in the middle of the hood. ■

"Flowing power moves direct from engine to wheels through double hydraulic torque converters. No conventional transmission or clutch, or conventional differential, either. Power goes to both drive wheels so it is impossible to be stalled by one wheel spinning on ice." That was just part of the advertising campaign for the Tucker '48. It has a 128-inch wheelbase, is five feet from road to roof, delivers thirty to thirty-five miles per gallon, can go from zero to sixty in ten seconds, and has an estimated top speed of 120 miles per hour. This "Car of Tomorrow" was the vision of Preston Tucker. The fastback sedan was styled by Alex S. Tremulis and put together by chief mechanic John Eddie Offutt. Only fifty-one of this remarkable car were made—forty-seven still survive—and luckily one of them is on display at the LeMay Museum in Tacoma. The Tucker '48 introduced features such as a laminated safety glass windshield and a safety frame surrounding the passenger compartment, and the conventional instrument panel was replaced by an attractive sponge rubber crash board cowl. ■

| Photo by **Alan S. Weiner** |

Dickman Mill Park occupies a nine-acre location that was home to Dickman Lumber Mill from the 1890s until 1974. Metro Parks acquired the site in the early 1990s, and Bruce Dees & Associates was retained to design the master plan and first phase of development.

Bruce Dees & Associates Plays Key Role in Revitalization

To paraphrase a local politician, "Tacomans have caught the renovation bug." The city's revitalization began in the 1980s, and Bruce Dees & Associates, which was founded in 1983, played a key role in many of the significant revitalization projects around the area.

When the University of Washington decided to add space by renovating the old warehouse district downtown, Bruce Dees, who is a Fellow with the American Society of Landscape Architects, was there as a member of the master plan design team. "Bruce Dees & Associates then created the construction drawings for pedestrian walkways, plazas, and landscape planting. We were very careful to preserve the details and the industrial character of the old buildings," said Bruce Dees, owner and Tacoma native.

Bruce Dees & Associates has played a major role in the revitalization of Tacoma's waterfront as well. Dickman Mill Park and Thea's Park restore vital shoreline for public access and recreation while maintaining a link to Tacoma's maritime and lumber industry past through design and interpretative elements.

In addition to their work on campuses and urban design, such as the Pierce County Environmental Services building and ball fields, BD&A's work can be seen in trails, community and neighborhood parks, and athletic fields throughout Tacoma and the surrounding areas.

BD&A has won numerous national and local awards for their innovative, environmentally sensitive designs.

The firm created the Wapato Hills master plan that led to the preservation of the eighty-three-acre open space in Tacoma's south end.

The Foothills Trail is a major project to convert twenty-six miles of unused railroad to a multipurpose trail. This ongoing project—being developed in phases—includes wetlands and river frontages, with numerous viewpoints and bridge crossings.

Another prime example of BD&A's work is the Nathan Chapman Memorial Trail. This multiuse trail links South Hill Community Park with Heritage Recreation Center, which was also designed by BD&A. Heritage Recreation Center is the newest and largest athletic complex in Pierce County. It is a partnership between Pierce County and the Puyallup School District. "The design was developed to accommodate both partners, teaching for the schools and recreation for the community," Dees explained.

BD&A has won numerous national and local awards for their innovative, environmentally sensitive designs. The Hood Canal Wetlands project provides interpretative trails for the North Mason School District. This project won two national awards, one from the Waterfront Center in Washington, D.C., and one from the American Society of Landscape Architects. The firm's projects have also received awards from the Washington Recreation and Parks Association every year since the beginning of their facility awards program.

BD&A has also done extensive design for the Boeing Company at several of their plants as well as Boeing's Commercial Airplane headquarters and campus.

Listing all BD&A's accomplishments would take far too long, but a drive around the city cannot fail to reveal their involvement in Tacoma. ■

Thea's Park is the terminus for the Thea Foss Esplanade which, when complete, will be the longest waterfront walkway in the nation. Bruce Dees & Associates designed Thea's Park and was a member of the Thea Foss Esplanade Master Plan Design Team.

The name "Tacoma" stems from the Indian name for Mount Rainier, Tacobet, which means "Mother of the Waters." Day or night, it is evident that water still plays a major role in the city's prosperity. Nestled on the shores of Puget Sound with Mount Rainier in the background, Tacoma lives up to its reputation as being one of America's most livable communities. It is conveniently located between the metropolis of Seattle and the state capital of Olympia. According to local sources, it is the "ideal place for people on the move because it has all the attractions of larger cities, but it still has a hometown feel." The port services over fifteen steamship lines, two transcontinental railroads, over two hundred inter- and intrastate trucking lines, and more than twenty air-freight forwarders. Since Nicholas DeLin shipped his first cargo from his mill down to San Francisco in 1853, the prosperity of the city has been linked to the waterfront. ■

THEA'S PARK

Dedicated August 1996

Park land acquisition and construction funded by:

Metropolitan Park District of Tacoma 1986 General Obligation Bond Funds

Washington Wildlife and Recreation Program grant monies from the
State of Washington Interagency Committee for Outdoor Recreation

General funds from the City of Tacoma

A land donation from the Port of Tacoma

Northwest TREASURE FEATURED COMPANIES

Brown & Brown Insurance
1301 A Street, Suite 200
Tacoma, Washington 98401-1718
253.396.5500
www.bbinswa.com

Insurance Provider (p. 92-93)
The nation's eighth-largest independent insurer provides its Tacoma–Pierce County clients with outstanding risk management and asset protection services. With a presence in the region that goes back over one hundred years, the firm also continues its mission to build a lasting legacy of community service and stewardship.

Bruce Dees & Associates
222 East 26th Street
Suite 202
Tacoma, Washington 98421
253.627.7947
www.bdassociates.com

Landscape Architect (p. 158-159)
Founded in 1983, Bruce Dees & Associates is recognized for design excellence in the Pacific Northwest. Their work integrates physical planning, urban design, architecture, and art, for park and athletic facility designs, as well as for waterfront and environmentally sensitive areas. They create healthful spaces with a timeless character that improves with age and use.

Cannon Construction
406 Porter Way
Milton, Washington 98354-9638
253.922.2787
www.cannonconstructioninc.com

Contractor-General (p. 14-15)
Since 1985 Cannon Construction has responded to the rapid changes in the telecommunications industry. As a telecommunications infrastructure and utility solutions company, Cannon Construction provides turnkey copper, data, and fiber cabling systems for corporations and government agencies worldwide.

Cascade Regional Blood Services
220 South I Street
Tacoma, Washington 98401
253.830.3200
www.cascadebloodcenters.org

Nonprofit Blood Service (p. 50)
Cascade Regional Blood Services has served hospitals in the South Puget Sound area and surrounding counties as an independent, volunteer-supported, non-for-profit blood resource since 1946.

Columbia Bank
1301 A Street, Suite 800
Tacoma, Washington 98401
253.305.1900
www.columbiabank.com

Bank (p. 112-114)
Columbia Bank is a Washington state–chartered, full-service commercial bank providing products and services to individuals, business, and the real estate community. A wholly owned subsidiary of Columbia Banking System, Inc. (NASDAQ: COLB), Columbia Bank operates over thirty branches in Pierce, King, Cowlitz, Kitsap, and Thurston counties.

Comfor Products, Inc.
2105 51st Avenue East
Tacoma, Washington 98424
888.291.1338
www.irfoam.com

Manufacturing (p. 102-104)
Since 1946, IR Specialty Foams has been the leader in specialty foam products, servicing a diverse client base in the civilian and government marketplace. The company is the oldest and largest fabricator of open-cell and closed-cell foam products in the Pacific Northwest. IR Specialty Foams is the parent company of Comfor-Pedic™, a manufacturer of specialty bedding—specifically, fabric-sided foam mattresses.

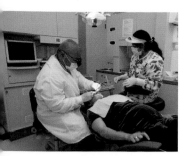

Community Health Care
101 East 26th Street
Tacoma, Washington 98421-1103
253.597.4550
www.commhealth.org

Health Care (p. 18-19)
A model of excellence in community-based, collaborative care, Community Health Care provides patients throughout Pierce County with high-quality, compassionate, and accessible medical and dental services, regardless of ability to pay.

Courtyard by Marriott— Tacoma Downtown
515 Commerce Street
Tacoma, Washington 98402
253.591.9100
www.marriott.com

Hotel (p. 138-140)
Located in the heart of downtown, the Courtyard by Marriott–Tacoma Downtown offers guests everything they've come to expect from a Marriott property, along with easy access to city sights and attractions.

DaVita, Inc.
1423 Pacific Avenue
Tacoma, Washington 98402
253.272.1916
www.davita.com

Health Care—Health Services (p. 60-61)
DaVita, Inc. is the nation's leading independent provider of dialysis services, providing care to more than 94,500 patients at 1,200 outpatient dialysis centers in 41 states and the District of Columbia, as well as with inpatient dialysis services in over 300 hospitals. In Tacoma–Pierce County, DaVita is one of the largest employers, boasting four dialysis centers and the company's main business office.

Franke Tobey Jones
340 North Bristol
Tacoma, Washington 98407
: 253.752.6621
www.franketobeyjones.com

Retirement Community (p. 78)
For more than eighty years, Franke Tobey Jones Continuing Care Retirement Community has offered independence, dignity, wellness, community involvement, and fun to seniors in the Tacoma area. From independent living, to twenty-four-hour skilled health care, Franke Tobey Jones stands for a tradition of excellence.

KeyBank
1101 Pacific Avenue
Tacoma, Washington 98411
253.305.7750
www.key.com

Bank (p. 144-147)
Cleveland-based KeyCorp is one of the nation's largest bank-based financial services companies. Key companies provide investment management, retail and commercial banking, consumer finance, and investment banking products and services to individuals and companies throughout the United States and, for certain businesses, internationally.

King Oscar Tacoma Inn, Motels & Convention Centers
820 South Hosmer
Tacoma, Washington 98444
253.539.1153
www.koscar.net

Hotel (p. 108-110)
The King Oscar Tacoma Inn, Motels & Convention Centers offer business and leisure travelers inviting accommodations and superior hospitality. The properties are all conveniently located in the Interstate 5 Corridor.

LeMay Enterprise, Inc.
PO Box 44459
Tacoma, Washington 98444
800.345.3629
www.lemayinc.com

Waste Removal Company (p. 124-126)
LeMay Enterprises is one of the largest and one of the few remaining family-owned refuse companies in the United States. Their total collection area extends from Mount Rainier to the ocean and from Puget Sound to the Cowlitz River with approximately 160,000 customers.

Milgard Manufacturing, Inc.
1010 54th Avenue East
Tacoma, Washington 98424
253.922.6030
www.milgard.com

Manufacturing Company—Windows and Doors (p. 52-53)
Milgard Manufacturing, Inc. is a premier provider of aluminum, vinyl, and fiberglass windows and patio doors and windows. With nineteen factory locations and more than five thousand employees nationwide, the company is able to offer truly customized service throughout the United States, enhancing homes with its extensive collection of high-quality products.

MultiCare Health System
300 Elliot Avenue West, Suite 300
Seattle, Washington 98119-4118
206.577.1803
www.multicare.org

Health Care (p. 22-23)
Encompassing three hospitals, physicians' clinics, urgent-care centers, and home care and hospice services, this community-based, nonprofit health-care organization provides compassionate, innovative care to patients throughout southwest Washington.

Pacific Lutheran University
12180 Park Avenue South
Tacoma, Washington 98447-0003
253.535.7354
www.plu.edu

College—University (p. 30)
Pacific Lutheran University is located in suburban Parkland, six miles south of Tacoma, on a 126-acre woodland campus that is truly representative of the natural grandeur of the Pacific Northwest. Serving more than thirty-six hundred students, PLU offers a full range of liberal arts and professional programs.

Pierce County Public Works & Utilities
2702 42nd Street, Suite 201
Tacoma, Washington 98409-7322
253.798.3159
www.co.pierce.wa.us

Public Utilities (p. 44-47)
The Pierce County Public Works & Utilities department is responsible for all transportation and environmental services for the county. In fulfilling these responsibilities to the citizens and the environment, the department is committed to providing service that is responsive, fair, efficient, and effective.

Port of Tacoma
One Sitcum Plaza
Tacoma, Washington 98421
253.383.5841
www.portoftacoma.com

Port (p. 82-83)
The Port of Tacoma is one of the leading international ports on the West Coast, handling more than $35 billion in global trade and more than $3 billion in Alaskan trade each year. Its imports include everything from automobiles and electronics to footwear, while its exports include plastics, grain, and more. A five-member commission, elected by Pierce County citizens, serves as the port's board of the directors.

Rainier Connect
805 Pacific Avenue
Tacoma, Washington 98402
253.683.4200
www.rainierconnect.com

Telecommunications (p. 116-117)
Rainier Connect, family-owned for five generations, is a telecommunications company that provides local phone, long distance, cable television, and high-speed Internet services to residential and commercial customers throughout Tacoma–Pierce County.

Russell Investment Group
909 A Street
Tacoma, Washington 98402
253.572.9500
www.russell.com

Financial Services Company (p. 26-27)
Russell Investment Group is one of the world's leading pension fund consultants with some $2.3 trillion under advisement. Investors in thirty-nine countries trust its legendary money-manager research and comprehensive knowledge of worldwide markets, which allow Russell to deliver exceptional strategies and insights.

Simpson Investment Company
917 East 11th Street
Tacoma, Washington 98421
253.779.6400
www.simpson.com

Wood Products Company (p. 96-97)

Founded in 1890, Simpson is one of the oldest continuously operating forest products companies in the Pacific Northwest. With headquarters in Tacoma, there are three operating subsidiaries: Simpson Timber Company, Simpson Door Company, and Simpson Tacoma Kraft Company, LLC.

Sound Credit Union
331 Broadway Plaza
Tacoma, Washington 98401
253.383.2016
www.soundcu.com

Credit Union (p. 152-153)

Sound Credit Union was formed in 1940 by employees of Pacific Telephone and Telegraph with a deposit of $106.50. Today the member-owned credit union has over thirty-eight thousand members and assets exceeding $285 million. It has ten branch locations in and around Tacoma and offers a full array of financial services.

Tacoma Community College
6501 South 19th Street
Tacoma, Washington 98466
253.566.5000
www.tacomacc.edu

College—University (p. 34)

More than seventeen thousand students choose Tacoma Community College each year as the place to begin their college education, earn an associate's degree, or train for a career. Specialized certificate programs and customized training solutions for business and industry bring a real-world focus to learning.

Tacoma Electric Supply, LLC
311 South Tacoma Way
Tacoma, Washington 98409
253.475.0540
www.tacomaelectric.com

Electric Supply Distributor (p. 86-87)

Distinguished by knowledgeable employees, loyal customers, and active community involvement, this family-run operation is now one of the top 200 wholesale electrical supply distributors in the country.

Tacoma Goodwill Industries
714 South 27th Street
Tacoma, Washington 98409
253.272.5166
www.tacomagoodwill.org

Nonprofit—Business Rehab (p. 36-37)

Tacoma Goodwill Industries is the largest Goodwill in the state of Washington. Founded in 1921, the not-for-profit organization provides vital job training, education, and employment for people with disabilities and disadvantages.

Tacoma Public Utilities
3628 South 35th Street
Tacoma, Washington 98409-3115
253.502.8277
www.tacomapublicutilities.com

Public Utilities (p. 72-75)

By overseeing the operations of three separate utility providers, this municipally owned and operated utility provides its Pierce County customers with reliable, safe, and high-quality electrical power, water, and freight rail services.

Tacoma–Pierce County Chamber of Commerce
950 Pacific Avenue, Suite 300
Tacoma, Washington 98402
253.627.2175
www.tacomachamber.org

Chamber of Commerce (p. 134-135)

The Tacoma–Pierce County Chamber of Commerce is one of the largest and most aggressive business organizations in the Northwest. Since its inception in 1884, the not-for-profit organization has been promoting economic prosperity and a strong business climate through advocacy, networking, resources, and business development services for its members.

TAPCO Credit Union
6312 19th Street West
Tacoma, Washington 98466
253.565.9895
www.tapcocu.org

Credit Union (p. 90)
TAPCO Credit Union is a nonprofit cooperative institution that has served the financial needs of City of Tacoma and Pierce County employees, as well as residents of Pierce County, since 1934. The organization, which boasts twenty-four thousand members and $190 million in assets, provides its member-owners with a full suite of accounts, loans, and additional financial services.

The Boeing Company
P.O. Box 3707, MC 21-70
Seattle, Washington 98124
206.655.2121
www.boeing.com

Manufacturing Company—Aerospace (p. 64-65)
Founded by William Boeing, this high-tech company has customers in 145 countries and supplies roughly 75 percent of the world's commercial jetliners. Boeing is also the largest private employer in the state of Washington with more than sixty thousand employees.

Totem Ocean Trailer Express, Inc.
32001 32nd Avenue, Suite 200
Federal Way, Washington 98001
800.426.0074
www.totemocean.com

Freight Company—Ocean (p. 120-121)
Totem Ocean Trailer Express, Inc., is the premier provider of ocean transportation to Alaska. The privately owned corporation operates a state-of-the-art fleet of Roll-on/Roll-off cargo ships between the Port of Tacoma and the Port of Anchorage, as well as providing overland highway and intermodal connections throughout greater Alaska, the lower forty-eight states, and Canada.

University of Puget Sound
1500 North Warner Street, Suite 1041
Tacoma, Washington 98416-1041
253-879-3100
www.ups.edu

University (p. 68-69)
With a curriculum that emphasizes critical thinking, discourse, and communication; a talented, multidimensional faculty; and an environment that fosters understanding of self and others, this nationally ranked liberal arts college prepares its students for a lifetime of productive leadership.

University of Washington, Tacoma
1900 Commerce Street
Tacoma, Washington 98402
253.692.4000
www.tacoma.washington.edu

University (p. 40-41)
A world-class university with a small-campus feel, the University of Washington, Tacoma brings expanded educational opportunities and mutually beneficial public-private partnerships to the South Puget Sound region.

Wells Fargo
1201 Pacific Avenue, 3rd Floor
Tacoma, Washington, 98402
253-593-5381
www.wellsfargo.com

Bank (p. 56)
In 1857 Wells Fargo Bank opened agencies in logging towns on the Puget Sound. Today across Washington, they have 151 banking stores, including 10 locations in Pierce County. One of Wells Fargo's most important strategies is to "out-local the nationals and out-national the locals."

World Trade Center Tacoma
950 Pacific Avenue, Suite 310
Tacoma, Washington 98402
253.396.1022
www.wtcta.org

International Trade (p. 130)
The World Trade Center Tacoma provides a host of services and connections for membership companies engaged in international trade and investment.

Northwest TREASURE EDITORIAL TEAM

Kimberly Fox DeMeza, Writer, Roswell, Georgia. Combining business insight with creative flair, DeMeza writes to engage the audience as well as communicate the nuances of the subject matter. While officially beginning her career in public relations in 1980 with a degree in journalism, and following in 1990 with a master's in health management, writing has always been central to her professional experience. From speechwriting to corporate brochures to business magazine feature writing, DeMeza enjoys the process of crafting the message. Delving into the topic is simply one of the benefits, as she believes every writing opportunity is an opportunity to continue to learn.

Rena Distasio, Writer, Tijeras, New Mexico. Freelance writer Rena Distasio contributes articles and reviews on a variety of subjects to regional and national publications. In her spare time she and her husband and three dogs enjoy the great outdoors from their home in the mountains east of Albuquerque.

Grace Hawthorne, Writer, Atlanta, Georgia. Starting as a reporter, she has written everything from advertising for septic tanks to the libretto for an opera. While in New York, she worked for Time-Life Books and wrote for *Sesame Street*. As a performer, she has appeared at the Carter Presidential Center, Callanwolde Fine Arts Center, and at various corporate functions. Her latest project is a two-woman show called *Pushy Broads and Proper Southern Ladies*.

Amy Meadows, Writer, Canton, Georgia. Meadows is an accomplished feature writer who has been published in a wide variety of local, regional, and national consumer and trade publications since launching her freelance writing career in 2000. She also specializes in producing corporate marketing literature for companies large and small and holds a master of arts degree in professional writing from Kennesaw State University.

Regina Roths, Writer, Andover, Kansas. Roths has written extensively about business since launching her journalism career in the early 1990s. Her prose can be found in corporate coffee-table books nationwide as well as on regionally produced Web sites, and in print and online magazines, newspapers, and publications. Her love of industry, history, and research gives her a keen insight into writing and communicating a message.

Jim Bryant, Photographer, Port Orchard, Washington. Bryant was raised a military brat and began taking pictures before he finished high school. He studied photojournalism at Syracuse University and has traveled internationally with the United States Navy. He has worked for newspapers in Florida, California, and most recently in Washington. Since then, he freelances specializing in all facets of photojournalism for books, international magazines and corporations. He lives in Port Orchard, Washington, with his wife and children. More of his work can be seen online at www.oz.net/~phojo.

Eric Francis, Photographer, Omaha, Nebraska. Francis was born and raised in Nebraska. Early on, he honed his skills freelancing for local newspapers, magazines, and commercial clients. Francis now also works regularly for some of the nation's largest and best-known magazines, newspapers, and wire services, covering news, features, and sports. He continues to make his home in Omaha with his son Mitch, his girlfriend Michelle, and her children.

David Gibb, Photographer, Jacksonville, Oregon. David was raised and educated in Rochester, New York. He now operates his studio out of the historic town of Jacksonville, Oregon. David has photographed for many local and national clients including Harry and David, Jackson & Perkins, Roper USA., Weyerhauser, Eastman Kodak, and Meredith Corporation. David can be reached at www.dgibbphoto.com.

Sonja M. Hall, Photographer and Writer, Tacoma, Washington. Hall is the director of the Media Center for Tacoma–Pierce County and communications manager for the Tacoma–Pierce County Chamber. She holds degrees in IAS–Mass Communications from the University of Washington and is a contributing writer for *Premier Home & Garden* magazine. Her external photography work includes corporate, wedding, dance, and events. Hall's corporate images have been published in Tacoma area newspapers, and in the reports and publications of various local companies and organizations.

Jackson Hill, Photographer, New Orleans, Louisiana. Hill is a New Orleans–based location shooter with extensive assignment experience worldwide. Jackson began his career as a photojournalist for daily newspapers in the American South. He now shoots annual reports as well as industrial and editorial assignments from the Canadian Rockies to the Gulf of Thailand. Jackson frequently shows his personal work, and samples can be seen at his studio's Web site, www.southernlights.com.

Joseph Parshall, Photographer, Olympia, Washington. A native of the beautiful Pacific Northwest, Parshall enjoys capturing local images "relaying the spirit through imagery." He is the founder and president of Atlantis Media Group. His photography work comprises commercial, portraits, theatre, dance, and events. Some of Parshall's clients include prominent companies, and venues such as Seattle's beautiful Benaroya Hall, Livingston Boats, Wedding Technologies Inc., and the Tacoma–Pierce County Chamber.

Alan S. Weiner, Photographer, Portland, Oregon. Weiner travels extensively both in the United States and abroad. Over the last twenty-three years his work has appeared regularly in *The New York Times*. In addition, his pictures have been published in *USA Today* and in *Time*, *Newsweek*, *Life*, and *People* magazines. He has shot corporate work for IBM, Pepsi, UPS, and other companies large and small. He is also the cofounder of The Wedding Bureau (www.weddingbureau.com). Alan has worked throughout the Pacific Northwest and the Carolinas on books. His strengths are in photojournalism.

Majestic

I t is a well-known fact that Mount Rainier is the crowning glory of Mount Rainier National Park. However, what is not so well known is the fact that Seattle and Tacoma got into a fierce competition over the name of the mountain. Captain George Vancouver named it Rainier after an admiral, but locals called it Tacoma, which was a term used to describe a snow-capped mountain. It was a U.S. senator from Seattle who got the U.S. Coast Survey to put "Rainier" on the map. Tacoma's legislators and business leaders tried for years to reverse the decision. Once they made it as far as getting a bill through the Senate, only to have it die in the House. It seems the main objection of the Seattle contingent to changing the name was the cost that would be involved in redoing all the signs and trademarks that carried the Mount Rainier name. ∎

About the Publisher

Northwest Treasure: A Photographic Portrait of Tacoma–Pierce County was published by Bookhouse Group, Inc., under its imprint of Riverbend Books. What many people don't realize is that in addition to picture books on American communities, we also develop and publish institutional histories, commemorative books of all types, contemporary books, and others for clients across the country.

Bookhouse has developed various types of books for prep schools from Utah to Florida, colleges and universities, country clubs, a phone company in Vermont, a church in Atlanta, hospitals, banks, and many other entities. We've also published a catalog for an art collection for a gallery in Texas, a picture book for a worldwide Christian ministry, and a book on a priceless collection of art and antiques for the Atlanta History Center.

These beautiful and treasured tabletop books are developed by our staff as turnkey projects, thus making life easier for the client. If your company has an interest in our publishing services, do not hesitate to contact us.

Founded in 1989, Bookhouse Group is headquartered in a renovated 1920s tobacco warehouse in downtown Atlanta. If you're ever in town, we'd be delighted if you looked us up. Thank you for making possible the publication of *Northwest Treasure: A Photographic Portrait of Tacoma–Pierce County.* ∎

BOOKHOUSE
GROUP, INC.

Banks ∎ Prep Schools ∎ Hospitals ∎ Insurance Companies ∎ Art Galleries ∎ Museums ∎ Utilities ∎ Country Clubs ∎ Colleges ∎ Churches ∎ Military Academies ∎ Associations